ESSENTIAL LEADERSHIP LESSONS

34 Characteristics FOR GODLY LEADERS

Richard J. Gehman

OASIS
INTERNATIONAL
PUBLISHING

Essential Leadership Lessons

ISBN 13: 978-1-59452-802-6
ISBN: 1-59452-802-0

Published by Oasis International Ltd, in partnership with Richard J. Gehman.

Oasis International is a ministry devoted to growing discipleship through publishing African voices.

- We ***engage*** Africa's most influential, most relevant, and best communicators for the sake of the gospel.
- We ***cultivate*** local and global partnerships in order to publish and distribute high-quality books and Bibles.
- We ***create*** contextual content that meets the specific needs of Africa, has the power to transform individuals and societies, and gives the church in Africa a global voice.

Oasis is: *Satisfying Africa's Thirst for God's Word.* For more information, go to oasisinternational.com.

Printed in India.

22 23 24 25 26 27 28 29 30 BPI 10 9 8 7 6 5 4 3 2

Table of Contents

Preface

The purpose of this book is to answer two basic questions: "What kind of Christian leader in Africa do we need according to Scripture?" and "How do we prepare this kind of Christian leader?"

For thirty-six years God granted me and my wife the marvellous privilege of training church leaders in Africa. For most of those years we served at Scott Theological College in Kenya. After training the students, we followed their lives with keen interest and prayers as they scattered throughout much of Kenya and into nine other African countries. We kept in touch with many. Over the years we worked with some and visited others in their ministries. With great joy and admiration, we observed many prosper and succeed in ministry, but with sadness we saw others stumble and fall.

Effective Christian leadership requires both character and competence. Almost none of the graduates failed because of incompetence. Whenever failure occurred, it was in the area of character.

Christian leaders are not limited to bishops and chairpersons. This book is designed for every Christian leader in Africa: the pastor, elders, and lay leaders of the local congregation; the overseers and heads of church districts, regions, and departments; the bishops of dioceses and denominations; teachers and principals in pastoral training institutions; and Christian leaders in para-church organisations. We may also say that since the fundamentals of Christian leadership are the same everywhere and for everyone, even Christian parents can benefit from the principles contained in this book as they lead and teach their children.

This is not a book on the theory of Christian leadership. It was born out of the practical experience of African leaders who have demonstrated Christian leadership skills. Two years prior to our retirement God gave the desire to visit as many of our Scott graduates as possible. What followed was one of the most memorable experiences of our entire lives. By God's grace I was able to visit over 175 graduates, mostly in their homes, all over Kenya, and together with my dear wife, we visited those serving in seven other countries in Africa. During our visits I interviewed each one to learn their experiences in ministry and the lessons they have learned. These interviews were transcribed onto 500 typewritten, single-spaced pages.

In 2008 a textbook of 335 pages was published by Oasis International based on those interviews and further research, entitled, *Learning to Lead: The Making of a Christian Leader in Africa*. This present book, *Essential Leadership Lessons*, is an abridged version of that book to make it more accessible to the average reader.

The notion of a *Christian leader in Africa* entails three ideas: leadership (role), Christian (character), and Africa (context).

LEADERSHIP

The role of *leadership* has been variously defined:

- The ability to make things happen (Ted Engstrom)[1]
- The ability of one person to influence others (Oswald Sanders)[2]
- Influence. Anyone who *influences* someone else to do something has led that person . . . *A leader takes people where they would never go on their own* (Hans Finzel).[3]
- Getting others to want to do something that you are convinced should be done (Vance Packard)[4]

CHRISTIAN LEADERSHIP

A *Christian* leader, however, is a particular kind of leader, a leader who emulates the Lord Jesus Christ. Christian leaders are servants of God who serve people in ministry. They are uniquely *servant-leaders* who seek to glorify Jesus Christ as they unselfishly serve Christ in ministry.

CHRISTIAN LEADERSHIP *IN AFRICA*

The principles of Christian leadership mentioned in this book are universal – they apply to Christians on all continents. But the context and application of these principles are with Africa in mind. Though the author is not an African, his whole ministry vocation has been in Africa. The book has grown out of scores of interviews with African leaders. You will hear African Christian leaders speak throughout the book.

Traditional African culture highly esteems the advice of the elders. A proverb of the Ngoreme in Tanzania says: "If you refuse the elder's advice you will walk the whole day." The Kiswahili version of this proverb says: "The person who does not listen to an elder's advice gets his leg broken."

The advice found in this book is offered by those Christian leaders in Africa who have learned by experience. We offer their counsel so that you need not walk the whole day or break your leg. As Solomon taught: "Listen to advice and accept instruction, that you may gain wisdom in the future" (Proverbs 19:20).

Acknowledgements

This book could not have been written without the valuable contributions of scores of people, especially the Christian leaders whom we visited and interviewed in eight different African countries. They included pastors, bishops, Bible school and college teachers and principals, Christian education directors, and church secretaries.

Abraham Chebunett
Abraham Koech
Agnes Kyalo
Agnes Kyengo
Agnes Mungwika
Alfred Muli
Amos Lwaya
Andrew Mulandi
Ann Nguku
Anna Ndebe
Alfred Dladla
Andrew Kendagor
Beatrice Kalya
Benedict Mutiso
Benjamin Kamende
Benjamin Mathaka
Bernard Nzioka
Bernice Njenga
Beth Njarambe
Catherine Ndeto
Charles Kababu
Charles Kimwele
Charles Muting'a
Daniel Kilonzo
Daniel Masesi
Daniel Muinde
Daniel Nungwana
David Kieti
David Mulwa
Dawit Yanna
Dinah Nyamai
Dorothy Obengo
Elijah Kalii
Elizabeth Timothy
Elizabeth Mutua
Emmanuel Falanta
Enock Shamapani
Ephraim Dlamini
Erastus Ngene
Esther Kibor
Eunice Bett
Fabian Maganda
Felicien Nemeyimana
Francis Kaunange
Frederick Mati
Geoffrey Muiru
George Opiyo
Gideon Karanja
Gladys Mpeta-Phiri
Isaac Kasema
Isaac Mulinge
Isaac Mutuvya
Isaac Mutwa
Isaac Simbiri
Hannington Kyengo
Jack Kamiruka
Jack Obongo
Jacob Kibor
James Kadanya
James Kombo
Japheth Muvengei
Jared Inzoberi
Jeddy Dladla
Jeremiah Muoki
Job Konzi
Joel Nyabinda
Joel Simbiti
John Karihe
John Moi
John Mondi
John Njoroge
John Njuru

Jonathan Maithya
Johnson Manda
Jonathan Mbuvi
Jonathan Mukote
Jonathan Mutunga
Joseph Imakando
Joseph Kahiga
Joseph Katwa
Joseph Kitur
Joseph Maswai
Joseph Mavulu
Joseph Mbunga
Joseph Ndebe
Joseph Onyango
Josephat Lumumba
Joshua Mutisya
Julius Kalya
Julius Musyimi
Julius Muthengi
Julius Mutwota
Justus Katoo
Justus Musyoka
Kamugu Mungai
Kibii Maiyo
Lawrence Bomett
Lillian Mwaka
Lydia Mwesa
Mary Mutetei
Mary Ndung'u
Mary Waita
Maruice Mpeta-Phiri
Mesfin Woldammanuel
Michael Mwaka
Michel Ngabonzima
Mike Mutua
Milcah Mukoma
Moses Njenga
Musa Magwesela
Mvula J. Mvula
Nancy Muli
Nathan Nzyoka
Nathaniel Kendagor
Ndeto wa Katunga
Noah Thananga
Pastory Masasila
Patterson Maimak
Paul Isayi
Paul Kisau
Paul Mutinda
Paul Njenga
Paul Ombati
Peninnah Kivunzi
Peres Akinyi
Peter Kitula
Peter Maina
Peter Mutisya
Peter Nakola
Peter Ngugi
Peter Ngule
Peter Njoroge
Philbert Nangale
Philip Muia
Philip Mutetei
Philip Osenya
Pierre Celestin
Rachel Ombati
Rebecca Celestin
Richard Muteto
Richard Sunza
Ruth Bomett
Samson Bett
Samson Jele
Samuel Gituka
Samuel Linge
Samuel Maritim
Samuel Munywoki
Shadrack Mukoma
Shadrack Mpanalehi
Shem Abuto
Silas Yego
Simeon Adera
Simeon Lellei
Simeon Otiende
Stanslaus Ndambuki
Stanley Mativo
Stanley Mutangili
Stephen Kitoo
Stephen Lentoror
Stephen Melly
Stephen Munyoki
Stephen Nduto
Stephen Sanya
Thomas Fumbuka
Timothy Kendagor
Timothy Mwangangi
Titus Kivunzi
Tom Obengo
Vundi Nason
Washington Were
William Kipkoros
Zipporah Wainaina

1

Advice from Christian Leaders in Africa

Church leadership takes many forms including elders, deacons, pastors, youth leaders, women's leaders, and Sunday school teachers. But usually, leadership is considered an office achieved by election or appointment such as chairman and chairwoman, superintendent, bishop, and other officials.

Every leader desires to be successful. No one wishes to fail. But success should not be measured by human opinion but by God's Word. Only God can give success and that is only possible when we play by God's rules. How can we please God and fulfil his purpose in our lives?

A total of 175 experienced Christian leaders (mostly pastors) were interviewed to learn practical lessons leading to success. This first chapter contains pithy comments on a variety of aspects of leadership.

Accepting advice from older, experienced Christians is vitally important. "Listen to advice and accept instruction," says Solomon in Proverbs, "that you may gain wisdom in the future" (19:20). "Give instruction to a wise man and he will be still wiser" (9:9). "Whoever gives heed to instruction prospers" (16:20, NIV).

THE SECRET OF SUCCESS

Why do Christian leaders succeed in ministry? To find out, I posed an open-ended question, "In your opinion, what are the three major reasons why people succeed in ministry?" In response more than 550 explanations were given. These were collated and assembled. Here are a few of the results. A fuller rendering is found in the book, *Learning to Lead: The Making of a Christian Leader in Africa* published by Oasis International.

Born Again and Called to Ministry

Not many mentioned this, but it is basic: "You should have the conviction that God has called you. Because of the things one goes through in the ministry, it requires a strong sense of call."

Dependence on God in Prayer with the Word

- Prayer! I don't see any other reason. Number two and three are still prayer. It is in prayer that you develop a deep relationship with God. You could include the Word of God. In prayer you talk with God. In the Word of God, he speaks to you. I see only prayer (and the Word). I have an open Bible when I pray so that the two go together.
- Personal devotional life! I noticed when I am going on well in personal devotions, the ministry also goes on well. One's relationship with the Lord.
- Intimacy with the Lord in prayer; walking with the Lord.
- I have not met anyone in ministry who is successful apart from prayer. I spend much time in prayer. In one week, I spend one day per week in prayer. I go to the top of the hill to pray and see God dramatically helping.
- At times I have felt, 'I know.' But knowledge has not made me succeed. But when I trust the Lord, I succeed. When called to ministry, there was no money for my education, but I went ahead anyway trusting the Lord. People advised me not to quit my work. No one supported me for fees. But I quit and went to Scott and God provided. I learned that when I trust God, he provides.

Faithfulness

- Faithfulness to God, to the ministry and to one's family were counted as very important in success. Half the respondents mentioned this essential.
- Faithfulness! That is the key. One may be godly but not faithful in preparation. Faithfulness in labour is rewarded.
- Faithfulness, both in money and in ministry! There are lots of temptations. No one supervises you. How do you use your time? Also, one should be faithful to your family, faithfulness in so many areas.
- Pastoral work is not like other work. It has no supervisor. It is you to plan visitation and time to study. One must be faithful to God.

Humility

Two-thirds of all respondents considered humility a most important character trait. This includes both being teachable and accountable. A whole chapter in this book deals with humility.

Teachable

- He must have a servant's heart.
- We tend to become bosses, instead of being servants.
- I see how I failed in humility. I failed to serve others. I feared to be seen last. I desired to be seen at the top. Servant leadership has given me the right perspective of all that is involved in leadership.
- You must be open to rebuke in order to learn.

Accountable

- You should not be on your own. You need to be accountable to God, to your superiors and to your wife. Don't act as though you are free in this world.
- Accountability especially in the area of finance! Groups of people need to be involved. One must be transparent. Even in life, one must be accountable.

Godly Character

Who a leader *is* is more important than what a leader *does*. Character is more important than skills in ministry.

- Leaders must lead by example. Those in a congregation will see him and watch him. This cannot be overemphasized. You are an example by what you say and do; for instance, one must be an example in your prayer life.
- You lead by your life.

Godly character in a leader is a reflection of God's character. This includes personal integrity, holiness of life, freedom from hypocrisy, sincerity of heart, and truthfulness.

Personal Integrity

- Personal integrity comes from the overflow of one's spiritual life. Once a leader's spiritual life goes down, his managerial skills and relationships also go down. You feel it if you preached a sermon in the power of the Spirit or if you preached it out of routine.
- We all need to work on this area of integrity in the areas of finance, women, and pride. This is a great need. I have seen many Christians and ministers have problems in this area. I knew a young pastor who is out of the ministry for seven years because of this. When one is caught with one of these sins, he is usually caught up with other sins as well.

Freedom from Hypocrisy

- There is a lot of hypocrisy in the church, a lot of pretence. People pretend. "I love you," they say. People show a different picture outwardly from what they are inwardly. We pretend to love, but we don't. Live what you preach; don't preach what you don't live.

Controlled by the Spirit

- Being led by the Spirit.
- There are divisions and in-fighting in the church, rushing to the courts or to the police to arrest a colleague. All this is due to church leaders not being led by the Spirit.

Truthfulness

- Speaking truth in line with the Word of God. Being truthful has really helped me in my ministry. If I speak the truth, it may create heat and conflict, but people know it and it heals.

Perseverance and Patience

- Bear with people. Be patient in serving. Some things are very hard.
- You need perseverance when things are difficult; you keep on going.
- You need staying power. There have been so many discouragements, but the Lord has kept me going. I should have quit a long time ago. The pastor has a very difficult ministry; so many do not appreciate him. What do you do? Quit? No, you stay.
- Be able to hold on and not give up. You need staying power.

Love of People

Interpersonal relationship skills are essential for success in leadership. At the heart of relationships is a deep love for the people you serve.

- People must feel the love of their leaders. They must love people. Leaders must always go the extra mile for people even when it hurts.
- One must love people, welcoming them without discrimination. They should have a burden for people. A "burden" is love shown in action.

SKILLS OF CHRISTIAN LEADERS

The question asked Christian leaders was open-ended: "In your opinion, what are the three major reasons why people succeed in ministry?" The vast majority of the answers dealt with the *spiritual qualifications of character*. Those who pointed to the importance of *skills in ministry* were surprisingly few. But ministerial skills are important.

In my own personal observance very, very few Christian servants fail because they lack skills for ministry. They fail almost always because they lack Christian character. It is that simple!

Nevertheless, skills are needed. Someone who is godly but who lacks leadership skills is greatly handicapped. As one person commented, "The gift of leadership is important for success. Many leaders are simply elected to the position because of wealth and relationships."

Christian Leaders Need Managerial Skills

Planning

- A visionary leader. One needs to have a vision.
- You need a dream. If you have no vision, you go in a vicious circle. To have a vision makes life exciting. You know where you are going. Working with people can be difficult when there is criticism, but you persist with your dream.

Decision Making

- Decisiveness in decision making, being firm about the decision, godly wisdom and discernment are important.

Organising

- You need to be organised and skilled in management.
- In ministry you need to plan and organise how you are to do the ministry.
- Periodic evaluation is needed after six months to see where you have succeeded or failed. Many pastors do not evaluate what they have done.

Delegation

- I've learned that it is so rewarding to equip people to do something, instead of doing everything myself. Don't get trapped in the busy syndrome.

Christian Leaders Need Leadership Skills

Leadership skills mentioned by these Christian leaders interviewed included diligence, self-discipline, motivation, enthusiasm.

CHALLENGES IN LEADERSHIP

> *Let us run with perseverance the race marked out for us, fixing our eyes on Jesus. For the joy that was set before him he endured the cross, scorning its shame, and sat down at the right hand of the throne of God. Hebrews 12:1b-2, NIV*

Serving the Lord in leadership positions is a glorious privilege and this privilege includes bearing the cross with Jesus who said: "If anyone would come after me, let him deny himself and take up his cross and follow me" (Matthew 16:24).

Everyone's cross is shaped differently just as the running lanes are marked out differently for each person. "The race marked out for us" may not be what we would choose, but Jesus Christ in his sovereign role as Lord of the church has called each of his children to run a particular race and carry a particular aspect of the cross he bore.

In preparing for ministry, we can benefit by being forewarned of the potential challenges facing us. Christian leaders were asked: "Describe one or more problems (challenges) you have faced in ministry which has caused personal pain." Following is a sampling of their replies.

Financial Challenges

- The most painful part is the finance. This causes us pain. We are paid so little that we cannot meet our needs. You are only given enough to eat today, and you do not know about tomorrow.
- One big problem uppermost is financial. It is a big problem to serve the Lord in church where you don't have support; it is every painful. What we receive is not enough for basic living expenses. You don't have enough to pay for medical expenses and education of the children. But God has helped us.

Relational Challenges

Although *finance* was the one word most frequently mentioned as a challenge, 67 per cent of respondents reported pain in relational challenges. These include:

Jealousy

- The greatest challenge is jealousy. People see your competence and they feel bad. They feel threatened, so they try to suppress and finish you.
- Opposition from church ministers is a major challenge. I noticed that education is very important, but the more you have, the more threatened some leaders feel.

Suspicion and Rejection

- It is a paradox. Graduates from upper-level schools preach nicely and people love them. But graduates from other schools feel threatened. I am not officially licensed yet after fifteen years of ministry. Others from low-level Bible schools are licensed to give Communion in two years. Then during church elections, they say I cannot hold office because I am not ordained.

Leadership Struggles

- Church politics with leadership struggles is so painful. When people colluded to say that I was not doing well, it was just for the purpose of protecting their positions. They sacked me, terminated my services from the church for fourteen months. It gave me great pain.
- There is a lot of church politics when one is a church leader; we are attacked. It was just the same with our Lord Jesus Christ who was attacked unreasonably.

Misunderstandings

A pastor's wife may be misunderstood because of the expectations of the elders. Fellow pastors may not understand each other because of different educational backgrounds. Elders may lack understanding of the pastor's vision or ministry.

Divisions

- Disagreements are a major challenge. There is always someone who has a contrary idea, especially among church elders.
- The division that occurred in our church caused me great pain. One thing that I thought we would always understand was that we should never take a Christian brother to court. This has caused me pain. It has affected my family relationships. It has affected me so greatly. At one point I thought it best to leave our church. Then I realized that there is no perfect church.

Hostility of Co-workers

- Opposition from my co-workers is a major problem. The people I thought would support me have not.
- Hostility from my co-pastors is a challenge. Some even hate me. They see my gifts and are jealous. I've been denied ordination. They fear that if I am ordained, I will get their seat. Laypeople want me to be ordained so I can marry them, but leaders oppose this.

Gender Challenge

- Because of my status as a single woman, people do not accept my recommendations. There is a gender problem in the church. They do not accept leadership positions for women. It is painful at times.
- In our churches people expect to be recognised for the work they do. But a lady graduate is not recognised. Their support is little compared to men.
- It is a bad experience to know that my boss looks down on me because I am a woman, and he thinks a woman cannot excel. It is a cultural thing to think that women are like children and cannot do anything worthwhile.

Other Challenges

- Sometimes you get so involved in the work that you almost become *lonely*.
- Some elders feel that *they know more than the pastor* and they challenge you in the ministry. It is not easy to work with elders. It has been so painful. Elders are strong on *tradition*.
- Our church always has people going to *councils*. But rarely do they put into practice or carry out the decisions of the councils. They just talk. Next time they talk around the same thing.
- The pain I have is *administration*. The spiritual aspect is overtaken by social activities. The emphasis is not on church growth or spiritual things but more on administration, councils, and finance. This is painful.
- There are *constant transfers* and changes of duties. If they see you excel and do well, they move you to a smaller church. When you are sent to a church, you want to start a project. Then you are plucked away prematurely. This is painful.

LESSONS LEARNED IN LEADERSHIP

These 175 church leaders were asked: "What practical lessons have you learned from these painful experiences?" Here is a sampling.

Perseverance

- God allows these things to make me trust him so that I will persevere.
- I've learned to be very, very patient.
- Endurance! Be slow to speak. Be patient and let God deal with the matter. Some things that seemed hard are now possible.

Trust in the Lord

- I have learned to trust God and to serve him despite people.
- One day I will face God and give a report. We trust in God for direction, what to do. He is our Supplier.
- When I look to myself, I can only be depressed. But when I look to the Lord and ask for his enablement, I find help. I go to him with a heavy heart, and he gives me joy.
- I have learned that the Lord will never leave me nor forsake me.

Prayerfulness

- The more problems, the more you depend on prayer. Prayer is essential. It is always my support. The more problems you have, the more you go down on your knees and pray to God.
- When you have problems, you move closer and closer to God.

Humility

- Humility has been a very tough lesson. By serving in a place where I am threatened and ostracised because of my tribe, I have been humbled more than ever before.
- I've learned to keep quiet. When co-workers oppose me, I don't oppose them.
- We should not assume we are learned. I have learned not to show myself as a threat. I serve humbly. I've learned to be so humble, so I can be of help to them. I try to be simple and cooperative. I have come not to threaten them but to be a co-worker.
- I've learned to work without someone recognising or appreciating what I do. I realized that they never tell you. The result of my work is not for the applause of people but for the praise of God.

Forgiveness

- From the human point of view, one can become bitter. The Lord taught me a lesson of forgiveness. I did not do anything wrong, but I will leave it to God. He is the righteous Judge. I felt peace in my heart.

- I've learned the whole lesson of forgiveness. I went through a period of disillusionment and trauma. But the Lord told me to forgive. I went to the chairman and told him I have nothing against him.
- Without love and forgiveness, it would be very hard to minister. Many [people] step on your toes and sin against you.

God's Faithfulness

- When we remain faithful to God, he will always remain faithful to us. Not only does he give me more, he gives me peace. You don't have enough, but you feel satisfied and settled. You can serve faithfully.
- Let them go into the field, not afraid of what they will eat. God is faithful. They should not doubt God. They have chosen a noble job. It is the highest calling one can receive. If I would start all over again, I would be a pastor again. I want to assure them that God is faithful. My wife and I can testify to this. We have never gone hungry.

CONCLUSION

God's call to serve him in Christian ministry is a high and holy calling, though it comes with challenges. Focusing on God is the key. As one church leader said: "If I would ponder the problems, I would not serve the Lord. But by focusing on God, we can serve cheerfully. The Lord has always been with us. We have never lacked."

2

Basics for Christian Leaders

To become an effective Christian leader, one must understand and follow certain basic issues that are foundational for all church leaders.

QUALIFICATIONS FOR LEADERS

The Bible lays out the qualifications for elders, bishops, and deacons in 1 Timothy 3:1-13; Titus 1:6-9; 1 Peter 5:1-5. These qualifications also apply generally to other leaders in the local church.

Character of Leaders

It is significant that the qualifications laid down for leadership are not primarily about skills or gifts but about *character*. The character of a leader is the foundation of leadership. Without godly character, the most gifted leader will fail.

Character is what you are when no one is watching. It is what you do in the dark. Character is not the same as reputation. Character is what you are down deep inside you, the core of a person, not what others think of you.

Following are the character qualifications for all Christian leaders.

A Christian Leader Must Have a **Reputation above Reproach**

Paul begins: "An overseer [bishop] *must* be above reproach" (1 Timothy 3:2, emphasis mine). This is a categorical imperative meaning, "It is necessary." He further adds, "He must be well thought of by outsiders" (3:7). In other words, a Christian leader must have the reputation by Christians and non-Christians as a person with blameless character. No hint of scandal, no reputation of character flaws should be found in a Christian leader.

A Christian Leader Must Be **Spiritually Mature**

Emotional and spiritual maturity is a prerequisite for effective leadership. "He must not be a recent convert, or he may become puffed up with conceit and fall into the condemnation of the devil" (1 Timothy 3:6). Paul adds, "And let them also be tested first" (3:10).

The reasons for this are obvious. Leadership is a test of one's character and maturity. How will he react to external criticism or adulations of praise? How will he respond to internal temptations of greed or lust? There is no substitute for spiritual maturity tested over time.

A Christian Leader Must Utter **Edifying Speech**

A leader with a loose tongue is divisive. He should not be "quarrelsome", "not [be] double-tongued [insincere]", and his wife must not be a slanderer. Words are powerful. They can build up or tear down. Once spoken, words cannot be taken back.

A Christian Leader Must Be **Self-Controlled**

A Christian leader "must be above reproach" (1 Timothy 3:2). He must be sober minded, self-controlled, not quick-tempered, not violent but gentle, and not a drunkard or addicted to much wine. A leader above reproach is one who exercises control over his desires. He controls his emotions and guards his words so that what comes out of his mouth is gracious and kind. He controls any impulse to be contentious, quarrelsome, or violent in words or actions.

A Christian Leader Must Be **Content**

A disqualification for leadership is "a lover of money" (1 Timothy 3:3). He must not be "greedy for dishonest gain" (3:8), and not even be "greedy for gain" (Titus 1:7). Leaders are often snared by their positions to misappropriate money for themselves. In other words, leaders are tempted to become thieves. Covetousness and greed are ancient temptations (see Ezekiel 34:1-10) and were present in the early church (see 1 Peter 5:2). In contrast, "Godliness with contentment is great gain" (1 Timothy 6:6).

A Christian Leader Must Be **Respectable in Conduct**

Christian leaders must be "respectable" (1 Timothy 3:2) and "dignified" (3:8). They should not be frivolous or childish. Instead, they should conduct themselves with dignity.

A Christian Leader Must Be **Sociable**

Love of strangers or being "hospitable" (Titus 1:8) is a further qualification.

A Christian Leader Must Be Faithful in Marriage

Christian leaders should be "the husband of one wife" (1 Timothy 3:2; Titus 1:6). Literally, this means he must be a *one-woman man* or a *man of one woman*. In other words, the leader should be faithful to his one wife. There should be no other woman in his life. This does not disqualify bachelors from being elders. It merely stresses the importance of a married man being faithful to his one wife.

Skills of Leaders

The emphasis in Scripture is on character, but two skills are mentioned.

Management Skills

A Christian leader "must manage his own household well, with all dignity keeping his children submissive, for if someone does not know how to manage his own household, how will he care for God's church" (1 Timothy 3:4). A father/husband is a manager of his household even as an elder/bishop is a manager in the household of God.

Teaching Skills and Knowledge of "the Faith"

Elders/bishops in particular are required to be skilful in teaching and with a firm knowledge of the faith. "He must hold firm to the trustworthy word as taught, so that he may be able to give instruction in sound doctrine and also to rebuke those who contradict it" (Titus 1:9). He should be a student of the Word with biblical knowledge and understanding in order that he might pass on the faith.

SPIRITUAL DISCIPLINES

Paul writes, "Keep a *close watch* on *yourself* [your character] and on the *teaching*" (1 Timothy 4:16, emphasis mine). It is not enough to be trained well in biblical theology and gifted in preaching. Charismatic preaching without character is a disaster. More leaders collapse and fail in ministry and more churches split and divide because of *character flaws* than for any other reason.

Leadership, whether you are an elder, Sunday school teacher, pastor, or bishop, places you in a vulnerable position. The greater one's sphere of influence, the greater will be the impact when mistakes in judgement are made or when sin is committed. Success in ministry requires the exercise of spiritual disciplines.

Mandate to Exercise Discipline

Paul instructed his minister in training: "Train yourself for godliness" (1 Timothy 4:7). The Greek word translated *train* came from the world of sports in the

Greco-Roman empire. It means literally *exercise naked.* Youth trained their bodies in gymnastic sports, such as boxing and running. They trained strenuously with naked bodies to avoid any impediments in their running.

Paul's command, *train yourself,* is in the present tense and indicates an ongoing activity. As any athlete knows, the body deteriorates when not routinely exercised. To be in top performance requires *continuous* bodily exercise.

Discipline and training to gain bodily strength and endurance has temporal value, but godliness has eternal value. As Paul stated: "*Train yourself for godliness*; for while bodily training is of some value, godliness is of value in every way, as it holds promise for the present life and also for the life to come" (1 Timothy 4:7-8, emphasis mine). For the sake of physical health, everyone should exercise the body (walking, running, and weightlifting), but discipline in training for godliness offers reward both for this life and the life to come. Daily discipline for godliness is essential for every minister.

> Do you not know that in a race all the runners run, but only one receives the prize? So run that you may obtain it. Every athlete exercises self-control in all things. They do it to receive a perishable wreath, but we [are] imperishable . . . *But I discipline my body and keep it under control, lest after preaching to others I myself should be disqualified* (1 Corinthians 9:24-27, emphasis mine).

Two required spiritual disciplines are talking to God (prayer) and letting God talk to you (meditating on Scripture). They go hand in hand.

Discipline of Prayer

Jesus was a Man of prayer! No one was busier than Jesus for he often had no time to eat (Mark 3:20). Yet in the midst of his heavy schedule of ministry he *made time* to pray. Mark records a whole day of ministry when Jesus was busy morning, afternoon, and evening. But the following day, "rising very early in the morning, while it was still dark, he departed and went out to a desolate place, and there he prayed" (Mark 1:21-35). This pattern continued throughout his life. Despite the business of ministry, "he would withdraw to desolate places and pray" (Luke 5:16).

The disciples of Jesus, especially those who are given responsibility of leadership in the church, must follow Jesus's example and do the same.

Prayer includes *worship* (adoring, praising, thanking God for all his mercies), *confession* (after self-examination, out of deep sorrow for sin, repenting, and confessing particular sins), and *petition* (as beggars, making our requests known to God with thanksgiving).

Discipline of Meditation on God's Word

Meditating on God's Word goes hand in hand with prayer. We need God's Word to show us how to pray. God speaks to us through his Word.

Sinful deeds spring from the human heart. "For out of the heart come evil thoughts, murder [hatred], adultery, sexual immorality, theft, false witness, slander" (Matthew 15:19) – the very sins into which Christian leaders fall. Transforming the mind (a crucial element of the heart) is necessary for godly living. That is why Solomon advises: "Above all else, guard your heart, for everything you do flows from it" (Proverbs 4:23, NIV).

Sin occurs through temptation and temptation *always* begins in the mind. For one to grow in godliness every disciple must engage in the transformation of the mind. This can only be done by the Spirit impressing God's will upon the heart and mind through the Scriptures.

Christian leaders need to *study* God's Word in order to teach the Word of God accurately. But Bible study can become academic and dry. While study is important, *meditating* on God's Word is essential. God blesses those who meditate on God's Word both day and night (Psalm 1:2). The goal should be to *apply* God's Word to one's life – to obey it. God commanded Joshua: "This Book of the Law shall not depart from your mouth, *but you shall meditate on it day and night,* so that you may *be careful to do according to all that is written in it*" so that you may prosper and have success (Joshua 1:8, emphasis mine). *Memorizing* Scripture is a powerful means of growing in godliness. "I have stored up your word in my heart, that I might not sin against you" (Psalm 119:11).

THE SOVEREIGN RULE OF GOD

Given all the changes which a Christian leader faces, what keeps the leader going? How does one thrive in leadership? A personal knowledge of Jesus Christ in saving grace is basic. Without a firm sense of calling to the ministry one will falter. The faithful spiritual disciplines of prayer and Word are non-negotiable.

But effective Christian leaders also manifest an unswerving trust in the lordship of Jesus Christ. They exhibit a confidence that Christ is the Builder of the church. God is in charge of every detail and is the Blessed Controller of our lives. Discouragement comes when the leader assumes responsibility for the building. Paul knew better. He commented, "I planted the seed, Apollos watered it, but God has been making it grow" (1 Corinthians 3:6, NIV). Christian leaders are only servants of the Lord, working in the Lord's vineyard.

Every student of the Word believes this in some measure. But it is in the details of life that doubts arise. Discouragement arises when pain is experienced: unbelievers are resistant to the gospel, new converts backslide, carnal Christians bicker and complain, a congregation fails to catch the vision of the leader. The list can go on and on: opposition, slander and backbiting, resistance, lack of cooperation, insufficient support, and unfair treatment.

In this section we will primarily quote the Scripture. Think long and hard on the Scriptures and apply them to your life.

God Is the Sovereign King

"The Lord has established his throne in the heavens, and his kingdom rules over all" (Psalm 103:19). "Our God is in heaven; he does whatever pleases him" (Psalm 115:3, NIV).

Think of this! If God is truly sovereign and does whatever pleases him, does anything take place in your life outside his control and will?

God Governs the Nations

"O Lord, God of our fathers, are you not God in heaven? You rule over all the kingdoms of the nations. In your hand are power and might, so that none is able to withstand you" (2 Chronicles 20:6). "For kingship belongs to the Lord, and he rules over the nations" (Psalm 22:28).

Think! Is God in control of every aspect of history? Of every detail?

God Uses Nations to Punish Others

"Woe to Assyria, the rod of my anger; the staff in their hands is my fury! Against a godless nation I send him, and against the people of my wrath I command him, to take spoil and seize plunder . . . But he does not so intend, and his heart does not so think; but it is in his heart to destroy, and to cut off nations not a few" (Isaiah 10:5-7).

Does God continue to use nations for his own purposes? Is God at work in the world today in every world event, fulfilling his purpose?

God Elevates Leaders and Removes Them

"It is I who by my great power and my outstretched arm have made the earth, with the men and animals that are on the earth, and *I give it to whomever it seems right to me*. Now I have given all these lands into the hand of *Nebuchadnezzar, the king of*

Babylon, my servant, and I have given him also the beasts of the field to serve him. All the nations shall serve him and his son and his grandson, until the time of his own land comes" (Jeremiah 27:5-7, emphasis mine).

"To the end that the living may know that the Most High rules the kingdom of men and gives it to whom he will and sets over it the lowliest of men" (Daniel 4:17).

Think about this! Does God raise up leaders in the church and remove them? Is God still the sovereign Lord who is control of everything today, even in the church?

God Overrules the Plans of Man

"The Lord brings the counsel of the nations to nothing; he frustrates the plans of the peoples" (Psalm 33:10). "Many are the plans in the mind of a man, but it is the purpose of the Lord that will stand" (Proverbs 19:21).

Did God overrule your plans or did others frustrate your good intentions? Can God's perfect will for your life be frustrated by others?

God Achieves His Purpose through Man's Sin

God Used the Jealousy of Joseph's Brothers to Achieve His Purpose

"And now do not be distressed or angry with yourselves because you sold me here, for God sent me before you to preserve life . . . So it was not you who sent me here, but God" (Genesis 45:5-8). "You intended to harm me, but God intended it for good to accomplish what is now being done" (50:20, NIV).

God Used the Jealousy of Jewish Rulers to Accomplish His Plan

"This Jesus, delivered up according to the definite plan and foreknowledge of God, you crucified and killed by the hands of lawless men" (Acts 2:23).

God Used the Injustice of Pilate and Herod to Provide Atonement for Our Salvation

"For truly in this city there were gathered together against your holy servant Jesus, whom you anointed, both Herod and Pontius Pilate, along with the Gentiles and the peoples of Israel, to do whatever your hand and your plan had predestined to take place" (Acts 4:27-28).

Does God continue to overrule the intentions of sinful men and use them to accomplish his purposes? Even in your life? Today? God's sovereign rule does not negate the importance of Christian leaders doing their best, but we rest in God's sovereign control over all things for his glory.

A FORGIVING SPIRIT

Learning to forgive is hard, but basic for all Christian leaders. Joy in ministry is inevitable for those called by God, except for the difficult people who will try you. They find fault and slander. Hard work is not appreciated but criticised. Self-willed, domineering people try the leader. As they say: "To dwell above with the saints in love, Oh that will be glory. But to dwell below with the ones I know, that is another story."

The natural response to difficult people is frustration, impatience, anger, bitterness, and self-pity. But if a leader is ruled by bitterness, grudges, and deep resentment, he or she cannot have an effective ministry.

What Is Meant by Forgiveness?

What Forgiveness Is Not

Forgiveness is not denying the offence nor denying the offender's responsibility. Neither is forgiveness a feeling. Forgiveness is not merely saying you forgive with the lips, for you must forgive from the heart. Nor is it a one-time event but an on-going process.

What Forgiveness Is

The Greek word conveys the idea of *letting go of a debt, releasing* as in releasing a prisoner. When someone forgives, he or she lets go of the offence and releases the offender. The English word carries the idea of ceasing to feel resentment against someone.

This means a forgiving person does not take revenge but instead shows kindness and compassion toward the offender. Instead of hating, the person loves. A forgiving person no longer brings up the matter to others and does not gossip about the offence. It is forgiven – the feeling of hurt is *let go* and *released*.

Why Should We Forgive?

Christ Commanded Us to Forgive

In the Lord's Prayer we pray: "Forgive us our debts, *as we also have forgiven our debtors*." Sin is like a debt. Jesus then explained: "If you do not forgive others their trespasses, neither will your Father forgive your trespasses" (Matthew 6:12-15, emphasis mine).

Jesus told a moving parable of a man who owed the king a debt that he could never pay: the wages for 60,000,000 days of working. When he could not repay it, the king ordered him, his wife, and children to be sold. The debtor fell on his knees and pleaded for mercy and the king forgave him his debt. But the forgiven man turned around and threatened a fellow worker who owed him the equivalent of one day's work. Falling to his knees the second debtor pleaded for time to pay the debt, but the forgiven man refused and threw the man who owed him money into debtor's prison. When the king heard this, he became angry and said: "You wicked servant! I forgave you all that debt because you pleaded with me. And should not you have had mercy on your fellow servant, as I had mercy on you?" (Matthew 18:23-35). The lesson is pointed! Because Christ forgave us, we forgive. A word to the wise is sufficient!

An Unforgiving Spirit Leads to Self-Destruction

Medical research has shown that unforgiving persons destroy themselves from within. They becomes captive to the endless cycle of reviewing the wrongs, leading to feelings of bitterness, resentment, self-pity, and ill-feelings.

How Can We Forgive?

Genuine forgiveness is the hardest thing to do, but the Christian leader is obligated to forgive, and he can forgive for Jesus's sake.

Experience the Forgiveness of Christ

The Bible teaches, "Forgiving one another, *as God in Christ forgave you*" (Ephesians 4:32, emphasis mine). "As God forgave you" is the key. Because God forgave us, we forgive others. In order to forgive others, we need to experience God's forgiveness.

Enter into the Feelings of the Offender

We need not agree with the motives of offenders, but to understand their thinking, to empathize with them, is a great help in feeling and showing compassion to them.

Demonstrate Love for the Offender

Love is primarily volitional, not an emotion. Forgiveness is not an emotion. If you wait for a feeling, you may never forgive. We are commanded to forgive. Show acts of kindness toward the offender and you will be surprised how you gradually come to sense in your heart the offence is gone. It is covered by the blood of Christ.

When Should We Forgive?

Unconditional Forgiveness

You cannot pass through life without offences coming your way. Paul alluded to this when saying: "Bear with each other and forgive one another if any of you has a grievance against someone" (Colossians 3:13, NIV). Annoyances and hurts are common. But unless the offence is so grievous that the offender should be confronted, we should unconditionally and unilaterally forgive.

Conditional Forgiveness

Some offences are more serious. Scandalous offences of breaking the Ten Commandments, like lying or committing adultery, must be confronted. Slander against fellow Christians can damage the unity in the body of Christ. This requires that the person be confronted following the principles laid down by Christ (Matthew 18:15-17).

Conclusion

Many blessings come when we humble ourselves and forgive others. As an African proverb says: "He who forgives ends the quarrel."

PERSEVERANCE OF LEADERS

Perseverance is crucial for the Christian leader to succeed in ministry. Without perseverance, a leader will eventually despair and give up. A Nigerian proverb says: "With patience you can even cook stones."

Perseverance among Successful People

Throughout history and in every profession, success has followed perseverance. Thomas Edison made 6,000 experiments over a period of two years before he invented the electric light bulb. Abraham Lincoln, one of the greatest presidents in the United States, failed in business and lost elections ten times from 1831 to 1860 before being elected as the president of the United States.

Perseverance among Christian Leaders

Here is what the African Christian leaders we interviewed said:

- There are painful things to the ministry, slander and rejection, but we need to look to God and keep on going. We need to persevere (pastor).
- Before people enter the ministry, they should prepare for action. The ministry is not easy with human strength, but with God we can make it. Ministry needs patience. I've learned the fruit of the spirit of patience (teacher).
- I've learned that if I am called by God, there is no quitting. Regardless of what comes my way – slander, suffering, discouragement, and unhappiness – I must not quit. One must not be distracted from my focus

which is on Jesus Christ. I must keep on going. This is not easy. To be a Christian – the name is a very nice word – but to live it is not easy. I must live the name I have. I must be serious with what I profess (teacher).

- There is need for patience and humility, because if you want things to happen quickly you will be discouraged because people may not understand the ideas you come up with and cannot accept them (pastor).

Patience Contributes to Perseverance

Patience is not identical to perseverance, but the two traits are interrelated because patience contributes to perseverance. Without patience, no one perseveres.

Patience refers to calm endurance and long-suffering whenever confronted with opposition, suffering, or provocation. *Perseverance* refers to steadfastness and persistence in following a course of action. Leaders who persist in their calling are patient when experiencing problems. You cannot have perseverance without patience. In fact, the Greek words for the English words *patience* and *perseverance* are the same.

One such Greek word is *makrothumia*, often translated "long suffering". Patience "suffers long" and refrains from anger whenever aggravated by people. Patient people are not easily provoked, and they don't erupt in anger with those who disagree with them. Patient people learned self-control. Paul urged the Christians in Ephesus to live "with all humility and gentleness, *with patience, bearing with one another in love*, eager to maintain the unity of the Spirit in the bond of peace" (Ephesians 4:2-3, emphasis mine).

Development of Perseverance

You cannot develop perseverance without being tested by all kinds of trials as James writes: "Consider it pure joy, my brothers and sisters, whenever you face trials of many kinds, because you know that *the testing of your faith produces perseverance*. Let perseverance finish its work so that you may be mature and complete, not lacking anything" (James 1:2-4, NIV, emphasis mine).

Trusting in the sovereign control of our loving God, James urges believers to endure trials of many kinds. Such trials should be seen as friends sent by God for our good. Even though trials may be frustrating, annoying, and even painful, believers should consider it pure joy.

Motivation for Perseverance

Why should we persevere? The motivation for persevering is twofold.

- Faith in the faithful God who is both good and sovereign in his perfect control of the difficult situations of life. All trials come from God's hand.
- Hope in the future reward at the return of Christ. Even as Jesus "endured the cross, despising the shame" because of "the joy that was set before him" (Hebrews 12:2), so the servant-leader endures much suffering for Christ's sake because of the joyful expectation of God's reward and future blessing.

James encouraged suffering Christians to persevere in their calling with reminders of farmers and of Job. After farmers plant the seeds, they wait with patience to receive a harvest. They exercise faith. Job suffered the loss of everything, yet he hung on to God in faith. God rewarded!

> *Be patient*, therefore, brothers, until the coming of the Lord. See how *the farmer waits* for the precious fruit of the earth, *being patient* about it, until it receives the early and the late rains. *You also, be patient* . . . As an example of suffering and patience, brothers, take the prophets who spoke in the name of the Lord. Behold, we consider those blessed *who remained steadfast.* You have heard of *the steadfastness of Job*, and you have seen the purpose of the Lord, how the Lord is compassionate and merciful" (James 5:7-11, emphasis mine).

3

Humility of Christian Leaders

Bernard of Clairvaux wrote in a letter to Aelred of Rievaulx that "The greatest virtue of the saints is humility."[5] To put it simply: without humility, no Christian virtue can exist. You cannot name any single virtue that thrives without humility.

Humility is a Christian virtue elevated by Jesus Christ. He frequently criticised the Pharisees for their pride because they did all their religious deeds to be praised by men. They loved to be seen praying, loved the seats of honour during feasts, and loved titles of honour. Instead, Jesus taught: "Whoever exalts himself will be humbled, and whoever humbles himself will be exalted" (Matthew 23:12).

After three years of being disciples of Jesus, James and John asked their mother to request for them the best seats in the Kingdom, seated on the right side and left side of Jesus (Matthew 20:20-21). Later, when the other disciples began arguing among themselves about who was the greatest, Jesus rebuked them saying: "Let the greatest among you become as the youngest, and the leader as one who serves. For who is the greater, one who reclines at table or one who serves? Is it not the one who reclines at table? But I am among you as the one who serves" (Luke 22:26-27).

Humility is not feeling inferior or being weak. Humility is being God-centred and God-conscious. Following are the characteristic traits of humility:

- Humility is unconscious of its humility. If a person thinks they are humble, they probably are not.
- Humility is remembering that the gifts we have come *through us*, but not *from us*. We have nothing that was not received from God.
- Humility does not seek to dominate, control, or manipulate. Humility does not strive for position and power.
- Humility is unselfish. The humble person is primarily concerned for the welfare of others, not their own. Humble people do not seek fame, look for better seats or better service, or desire fancy offices and lofty titles.

- Humility responds to criticism with grace, without defensiveness. Humility is open to correction and rebuke; it never takes revenge.
- Humility understands our own sins are worse than others.

When seeking the counsel of African Christian leaders, we found that they ranked humility as one of the most important character traits of a leader. According to them, humility is manifested in the following ways:

- *Admit making mistakes.* "When someone goes wrong, you must be humble enough to say, 'I'm wrong.' You need to take responsibility. Remember, you are a human being. You make mistakes too."
- *Listen to every person.* "A leader must listen to other people's viewpoints first because it is very possible in an African context, once the leader says something, the discussion is finished. No one else wants to say something. So the leader must be humble enough to listen to even the smallest viewpoint in coming to resolutions before stating your own viewpoint. Be careful not to be a dictator. Be open to other people's opinions."
- *Never boast.* "Leaders should not boast. If there is any praise, let others speak it. Once you boast, the chances of falling are great."
- *Never be proud of your education.* "Training should not make you puffed up, thinking that people will accept you more than those without training. One must not be aloof. You must mix with them."
- *Come down to the common person.* "Humility is the key. People fear learned people. We need to come down and follow Jesus. Humble yourself before others. Follow the example of the Lord (Philippians 2). Serve under the District Chairman who may be trained at a low-level Bible school. This is crucial."
- *Move slowly in making changes.* "They should be ready to work with people. They should implement slowly, and they will succeed. Those who go to church to change things, those who think they have excellent knowledge and others know little, they end up in conflict. They should deliberately bend to the level of the people."
- *Serve others as a leader.* "Once you are a leader in Africa, it is a position of honour. But one must be a servant. Leadership is serving others – serve others like Jesus Christ when he came not to be ministered unto but to minister. He humbled himself even to the point of the cross."
- *Avoid power struggles.* "I've seen many leaders being proud. But being humble brings unity. When you are down, others see that you are not competing for their seats. Then you can serve. Don't fight for position."

- *Be patient when others humiliate you.* "I found it very helpful, though not easy, to remain quiet when being humiliated. I chose to be silent and speak when I must, especially when things were going wrong. Those who were my enemies provoked me to speak. Then they found reason to accuse me. I learned it best to be patient."

THE PROBLEM OF PRIDE

Pride is the cardinal sin which damns the human race, because pride exalts self and is the root for all other sins. Pride is universal among all peoples including the westerners and easterners, British and Americans. The same is true of Africans whether Gikuyu or Maasai, Swazi or Tonga, Somali or Turkana. They all believe that humility is cowardice and therefore weakness.

Pride is not a specialty of any race or culture. All cultures, being the products of proud human beings, are expressions of proud people. Cultures provide differing channels for proud people to express their true self-interests. In Western countries pride is more individualistic, flaunting oneself before the neighbours with bigger houses and better cars, all in the attempt to magnify one's elevated significance above others.

African society is stratified with peoples ranked in different age groups. Those in a low social rank may be mistaken as humble individuals because they are only behaving according to the demands of society for that rank. Children are very subservient; adolescents are modest before their elders. Leaders may appear to be humble in the early stages, but as they gain rank they begin to behave according to the entitlement of their rank. When a man marries and has a growing family, when he is granted positions in the church as chairman or secretary or bishop, his self-image changes. He begins to claim the rights and entitlements to that position. Character traits of pride include the following:

- Pride is exalting self, receiving the honour belonging to God alone.
- Pride is the excessive belief in one's own ability that does not recognise God as the source of those abilities.
- Pride is self-exaltation in contempt of God. When we become self-centred and focus on self, comparing ourselves with others, we become puffed up, conceited, and blinded to our own weaknesses.
- Pride is idolatry, for in the final analysis it makes self into a god to be praised, adored, honoured, and served.

- Pride is the feeling of being superior to others: "I am better than . . . I am better educated than . . . I have more experience than . . . I have a higher office than . . ."
- Pride is the feeling of being entitled to something: I deserve more than . . . I deserve a better salary than . . . I deserve a better seat than . . . I deserve more respect than . . ."

The church leaders whom I interviewed, gave the following signs or evidence of pride among Christian leaders today:

- Struggling for leadership and power, using bribes and campaigning
- Public giving of contributions in *harambees* so as to be seen. When offerings are not announced publicly, they contribute little.
- Assigning others to do manual work in church while they stand and watch, or pretending to work with meaningless activities
- Not serving in church without pay, a love of money
- Desiring to be served rather than serving
- Flaunting oneself before the congregation by giving yourself as an example of some good work
- Overruling the wishes of the people and making decisions without consultation. "I am the chairman of . . . and so I have the final say."
- Flaunting education and degrees
- Believing they are *big people*, they have no time to *go down* to minister to the poor. They only associate with their own class.
- Desiring people with problems to come to them rather than the leader stooping down to go to them. This enhances their position.
- Desiring to be recognised whenever they attend meetings
- Wanting to be boss, they divide the church with their pride.
- Boasting of their influence and respect they have in the congregation, and the big size of the churches they are leading
- Bragging and telling people of personal and family achievements.
- Adopting big names such as prophet, apostle, or miracle worker; being ordained as a reverend and looking down on pastors and evangelists who are not ordained.

When the devil tempted Eve in the Garden of Eden to eat of the forbidden fruit, he said: "God knows that when you eat of it your eyes will be opened, and *you will be like God, knowing good and evil*" (Genesis 3:5, emphasis mine). Pride is exalting one's will above God's will. Because Eve was not content with God's gracious provisions in the Garden, she and Adam asserted their own will over God's will.

Elevating self and becoming little gods has been the vocation of humans ever since, taking credit for all the good in their lives and feeling superior. The tragedy is that pride has destroyed many Christian leaders. It is a sin which must be resisted at all costs. Pride is subtle and leaders fall into this trap without realizing it.

HUMILITY IN LEADERSHIP STYLES

Humility should transform any Christian style of leadership into a servant-leadership, following the example of Jesus Christ.

A leadership style is the way a leader carries out the function of leading. Leadership styles are determined by the personality of the leader and the history, traditions, and culture of the people he or she leads.

Traditional Leadership Styles

Leadership styles in the West range from authoritarian where the leader is dominant to hands-off where the worker is dominant. Variations of these extremes occur if the leader consults the workers or if the workers participate in decision-making.

The Chinese leadership style is primarily authoritarian. Confucian values with filial piety and deep respect for the elders in the family has extended to subservience to regional leaders, the emperor, and the president of China.

Traditional African styles of leadership range from top-down leaders (the *big man* rules) to bottom-up leaders. Many African societies were ruled by a centralized authority such as kings or chiefs who inherited their role. Leadership was considered absolute and incontestable. But numerous small African societies lacked central authority where kinship played an important role. Many African communities were governed by *group democracy* where leaders earned their position of leadership and performed their leadership roles within a council of elders.

The colonial legacy introduced an alien form of leadership. The African chief, appointed by the colonial authorities, no longer was guided by a council. He was no longer responsible to the people, but to the colonial government. Instead of leading through participation with the advice of a council of elders and accountable to the people, the African chief under colonialism ruled unilaterally with power. He was only responsible to the colonialists, not to the people.

This top-down, authoritarian, *big man* leadership style, so common in most cultures worldwide, has seeped into the churches. Cultures have profoundly influenced Christian church governments. The early Christian church adopted the hierarchical leadership style of the Roman Empire resulting in an infallible Pope at the top and authoritarian bishops below him. The Korean church, influenced by the Confucian teachings which shaped Korean culture, is led by authoritarian pastors who exercise strict control over the members.

The same is tragically true of many African church leaders. Growing out of the tradition of a hierarchical society and the *big man* chief of colonialism, the pastor and church leaders assume positions of authority. They demand respect even if not earned. They expect to be served rather than serve. Elders are never wrong. A hierarchy of leadership is common.

Biblical Leadership Style

It would be difficult to claim from Scripture a single leadership style. But the Word of God is clear on one thing. Whatever leadership style one chooses, *servant-leadership with humility* should characterize all Christian leadership. From the teaching and example of Jesus, *service* and *selflessness* should mark all Christian leadership styles.

Jesus described two contrasting leadership styles – those who serve others and those who lord it over others. Listen to Jesus's rebuke of his disciples:

> You know that those who are considered rulers of the Gentiles lord it over them, and their great ones exercise authority over them. But it shall not be so among you. But whoever would be great among you must be your servant (Mark 10:42-43).

The Bible presents two kingdoms: the kingdom of light and the kingdom of darkness, the kingdom of God and the kingdom of Satan. Conversion marks the change from Satan's rule to the rule of the Lord Jesus Christ. Salvation involves confession with the mouth that Jesus Christ is Lord and belief in the heart that God raised him from the dead (Romans 10:9). There is no salvation unless belief in Jesus Christ as your Saviour is accompanied by a sincere desire to follow Jesus Christ as your Lord.

The great leaders of redemptive history were known as *servants* of the Lord. The greatest figure in the Old Testament was Moses. When he died, the people could have remarked, "Moses, the Lord's miracle worker, is dead," or "Moses, the Lord's statesman, is dead," or "Moses, the great law-giver, is dead." Instead, God told Joshua, "Moses *my servant* is dead" (Joshua 1:2, emphasis mine). God called all the Old Testament prophets "my servants, the prophets".

Servant-leadership is not a weak leadership style. Cultural features of leadership style can be adopted by the church if they are not contrary to biblical principles.

But a truly Christian leader should be a servant-leader who is a bond servant of Christ, obeying and glorifying God in all things, and serving the people of God rather than seeking personal gain.

Human nature is intrinsically selfish, self-centred, and proud. All cultures reflect human nature and reinforce the desires of the human heart. But it is the responsibility of the Christian leader to follow the example of Christ.

SERVANT LEADERSHIP

Can a leader be a *servant*-leader? This idea seems like an oxymoron, an apparent contradiction. How can a leader be a servant? Few want to serve, but many want to lead. Yet the idea of a *servant-leader* is as old as the Bible, even though the term was first coined in 1970.

Meaning of Servant-Leader

Servant-leadership is perplexing to many because leadership bestows power, influence, and authority. Leaders achieve status and prestige. They do not think of themselves as servants. A servant-leader has power, but it is a certain kind of power exercised with humility. Worldly power demands and dictates. Spiritual power is soft and humble. So, what is a servant-leader?

Servant-Leaders Are Bondservants of the Lord

The principal significance of servanthood in the Old Testament is *submission* to the master. A Christian leader is a *servant of God.*

Servant-Leaders Serve God's People

Leadership is about someone's *role* among people. By definition, a "leader" is a person who leads, guides, directs, and is the head. "Servant" on the other hand is about *character.* The leader leads with *humility.* In contrast to the non-Christian leaders who rule over others, a Christian leader leads with a spirit of humility.

Characteristics of a Servant-Leader

The Servant-Leader Acknowledges and Practices Dependence on God

Education is important to grow competent leaders. Developing confidence is desirable. But a subtle danger arises when the leader becomes *self*-confident. Yes, there is a measure of self-confidence which is gained through education and experience. Capable leaders know what to do and how to do it. But self-confidence can grow into *self-reliance*, depending on oneself and not on God. A genuine servant-leader does not rely on her or his own knowledge and skills but on God.

The Servant-Leader Is Motivated by the Glory of God

The focus is not on self but on the glory of God, loving him, and obeying him in all things. In this the servant-leader is humble. "Whatever you do, do all to the glory of God" (1 Corinthians 10:31). In many traditions pride is achieved through leadership. A person is recognised and made famous because of leadership. This tradition has been brought into the church and leads to infighting for seats on the councils. But a servant-leader is one whose whole ambition is to serve the Lord and give God all the glory.

A Servant-Leader Hopes and Trusts in God

Confident in the sovereign rule of the Lord, a servant-leader knows that "for those who love God all things work together for good, for those who are called according to his purpose" (Romans 8:28). Instead of fearing those who may challenge their position, a servant-leader rests in full hope and confidence in God whom he or she serves. Many pastors and church leaders feel like quitting from time to time. The work is endless and thankless, the people lack appreciation, criticism is rampant, and jealousy and division hurt. But those who wait on the Lord, trusting in him, find their strength renewed.

The Servant-Leader Exercises Power through Weakness

The thirst for power has shaped the history of this world as leaders fight for more power. But Paul wrote, "We have this treasure in jars of clay, to show that the surpassing power belongs to God and not to us" (2 Corinthians 4:7). God works through human weakness and limitations. To keep Paul from becoming proud, God gave him a thorn in the flesh to remind him of his weakness. When Paul pleaded three times to remove the thorn, God replied: "My grace is sufficient for you, *for my power is made perfect in weakness*" (2 Corinthians 12:9, emphasis mine).

The Servant-Leader Develops Transparent Relationships

Cultural leaders separates themselves from others. Distance protects them from scrutiny. People do not see their blemishes because they avoid mingling with others. But Christian leaders are *among* those they lead, not *over* them. They live a transparent life and are held accountable by those whom they serve. Christ is our example to follow. He identified with those whom he would save and became one with them. So should servant-leaders.

The Servant-Leader Mentors Others for Ministry

One of the greatest leadership failures is failure to mentor others to become leaders. Many feel threatened when others do well. But *success without a successor is failure.* A servant-leader is not bothered by jealousy. Investing in others and preparing them for leadership is a true characteristic of servant-leaders.

THE SUPREME MODEL OF HUMILITY

Jesus not only taught us to be servant-leaders; he lived as a servant-leader. Jesus is our perfect model. For anyone to be a disciple of Christ, that person must submit to Christ's lordship. As James Hudson Taylor famously said: "There can be but one lord, and . . . those who do not make God Lord of all do not make him Lord at all."[6]

Jesus's Example of Humility

Jesus Washed His Disciples' Feet

Just before Christ's death, he met with his disciples in the upper room to celebrate the Passover (Mark 14:15; Luke 22:12). It was customary for a servant to wash the feet of the guests before a meal because feet became weary and dirty after walking the dusty paths. But no servant was found in the upper room and no disciple was willing to humble himself to wash his fellow disciples' feet (John 13:1). This was a lowly task.

So Jesus took off his long, flowing outer garment and took a towel and tied it around his waist. He stooped down and washed the dirty, stinky feet of his disciples, wearing only a loincloth, just like a menial servant. When he finished this graphic demonstration of humility, he said:

> Do you understand what I have done to you? You call me Teacher and Lord, and you are right, for so I am. If I then, your Lord and Teacher, have washed your feet, you also ought to wash one another's feet. For I have given you an example, that you also should do just as I have done to you (John 13:12-15).

To *wash one another's feet* means the disciples of Christ are obligated to offer others the lowliest of service from hearts of love and humility. Every Christian is responsible to do this, but especially Christian leaders who are examples for the flock whom they serve.

Jesus Died on the Cross

The greatest example of humility given to humankind was the humbling of Jesus "by becoming obedient to the point of death, even death on a cross" (Philippians 2:8). When writing to the church in Philippi, troubled by divisions and conflict, Paul wrote these profound words which are here quoted from *The Message* (a Bible paraphrase):

> Agree with each other, love each other, be deep-spirited friends. Don't push your way to the front; don't sweet-talk your way to the top. Put yourself aside, and help others get ahead. Don't be obsessed with getting your own advantage. Forget yourselves long enough to lend a helping hand
>
> Think of yourselves the way Christ Jesus thought of himself. He had equal status with God but didn't think so much of himself that he had to cling to the advantages of that status no matter what. Not at all. When the time came, he set aside the privileges of deity and took on the status of a slave, became *human*! Having become human, he stayed human. It was an incredibly humbling process. He didn't claim special privileges. Instead, he lived a selfless, obedient life and then died a selfless, obedient death – and the worst kind of death at that – a crucifixion (Philippians 2:2-8, MSG).

Paul gave this graphic example of Christ's humility in order to shame the Christians in Philippi who were acting selfishly and causing divisions.

Becoming Like Christ in Humility

Based on the example of Christ's humility, Paul pleads: "Have this mind among yourselves" (Philippians 2:5). Literally, Paul is saying, "*Keep on thinking* this among yourselves." It is a command to keep on thinking this way. The only way to develop a mindset of humility is continual practice – *keep on thinking* this way among yourselves until it becomes a fixed attitude and mindset.

This entails a spiritual exercise to become Christ-like. It involves prayerful meditation on Scripture. Human nature is self-centred, but Christ was other-centred. Servant-leadership begins in the mind. "Do nothing from rivalry or conceit, but in humility *count others more significant than yourselves*" (2:3, emphasis mine). Become conscious of your need to do this. Become aware of the times when you fail. If need be, confess to others. At the very least, confess to God and seek his help in following the example of Christ.

This has nothing to do with self-depreciation which is unhealthy. But we need to recognise that all we are is by God's grace. Though God has gifted us, the sun does not rise or set on us because we are extremely limited. Surprisingly, others are also gifted and capable! Besides, it is a command. Do it! "Count others more significant than yourselves." Take practical steps by obeying Philippians 2:4, "Let each of you look not only to his own interests, but also to the interests of others." If this command were easy, it would be commonly practised after 2,000 years. If it were impossible, God would never have given this command. And it all starts with *agape* love.

The rewards are enormous, both in this life and in the life to come. When a leader behaves as a servant-leader, people will notice and appreciate it. Though people are proud, we instinctively dislike arrogant people. We take notice of those who are kind, thoughtful, and unselfish, and we admire them. A servant-leader gains respect in this life. Apart from what others say or think, God promises a great reward. "Clothe yourselves, all of you, with humility towards one another, for '*God opposes the proud but gives grace to the humble.*' Humble yourselves, therefore, under the mighty hand of God so that *at the proper time he may exalt you*" (1 Peter 5:5-6, emphasis mine).

4

Love of Christian Leaders

You shall love the Lord your God with all your heart and with all your soul and with all your mind. This is the great and first commandment. And a second is like it: You shall love your neighbour as yourself of God. – Matthew 22:37-39

SELF-ESTEEM IN LEADERS

Life is not about you, neither is the ministry about you. The ministry is all about God who created you for his glory. *Everything* centres on God.

The paradox is this: when God is the centre, you are affirmed, but when you are the centre, you lose your self-esteem.

Put another way. When the greatest commandment is first, and when the second commandment is second, God will affirm you. But when self is first, you lose all sense of self-worth because a person's worth is in his or her relationship with God. To be an effective Christian leader one must have a healthy self-respect in order to reach out to others with love. Interpersonal relationship skills are fundamentally all about love.

Creation and the Fall

The epitome of God's creation in our universe was the human race. Adam and Eve were made in God's image. They became image-bearers, not carbon copies or "little gods," but a reflection of God. They reflected God in their personalities with life, intelligence, a will with purpose and decision-making capacity, self-awareness, emotional capacity, and spirituality.

This made possible a personal relationship with the Creator. As God's children they respected, loved, and adored their heavenly Father, and they submitted to God's will. In this condition Adam and Eve were granted dignity and honour in their personal relationship to the eternal God, always dependent on and obedient to him as God loved them and cared for them.

Everything changed when Adam and Eve proudly chose to become little gods, making their own decisions, independent of God. Through this disobedient act of the first man and woman, the human race was plunged into death, both physical and eternal. Sin also brought chronic anxiety.

The root of our chronic anxiety is alienation from God with feelings of guilt and shame, and this leads to low self-esteem and feelings of being unhappy, anxious, and alone. To enhance self-worth and feel better, people acquire wealth, power, and a name, instead of becoming reconciled to God.

Low Self-Esteem

The root cause of low self-esteem is the sin and guilt that has estranged people from God. Even those who have been redeemed suffer from the Fall because they do not have that relationship with God of perfect trust and obedience. Furthermore, a low self-esteem is learned through negative experiences when parents and others criticise, shame, reject, and scold a child repeatedly. A person who experiences rejection instead of warm acceptance, will develop an even greater sense of low self-esteem.

A person with an inferiority complex may not be inferior at all. He or she may be intelligent, physically attractive, and gifted, but *feels* inferior. He or she may feel depressed, lacking inner peace and joy. Self-criticism, self-hatred, and self-rejection are common.

Growing in Self-Esteem

Several steps should be taken to overcome a feeling of inferiority with its lack of self-esteem.

Grow in Your Relationship with God

Basic to everything else, a person struggling with feelings of inferiority must grow in the knowledge of God through persistent, faithful meditation on God's Word with memorization. Accept yourself as a child of God, forgiven and loved by God. In humility confess your sins and embrace God's forgiveness. Experience God's love.

Grow in Your Acceptance of Yourself

Certain things in life should not be accepted, such as moral weakness, laziness, ignorance, and lack of self-discipline. But many things are out of your control including your parental upbringing, physical appearance, intelligence, and opportunities in life.

Every person is granted certain gifts. No one is excluded. Learn to accept yourself as you are. Since your self-rejection is the result of years of negative experiences, you need to make it a practice to thank God repeatedly for those gifts he has given and accept yourself as from his hand.

Grow in Your Affirmation of Others

A healthy self-image does not dwell on self but on others. Affirm others, congratulate them, praise them, thank them, and help them. As you do this, others will become your friends and they will begin to fill your emotional cup with acceptance. The more you are loved, the more you gain self-esteem, and the more you can love.

An Ewe-Mina proverb says, "The dog does not worry when the chicken runs over to the bones." A person who feels secure will not feel threatened by the performance or gifts of others. When your cup of God's love is full and overflowing, you can pour out love to others. In contrast, a jealous person is self-centred and therefore cannot love others.

JEALOUSY: THE OPPOSITE OF LOVE

"Love does not envy" (1 Corinthians 13:4). An African proverb says: "Peace is good soil for man to grow." Love provides peace but jealousy destroys it. Solomon said: "Envy makes the bones rot" (Proverbs 14:30). A Kenyan proverb says: "Lack of unity spells weakness;" and a Swahili proverb says: "Unity among the cattle makes the lion lie down hungry." Unity is impossible where jealousy reigns. What is needed is a united community bound together with love.

Godly Jealousy

Jealousy can be either good or bad. Humankind, created in the image of God, has the capacity for the emotions of jealousy and anger since God is a God who displays jealousy and wrath. In the midst of renewing the Ten Commandments, God warned Israel: "For you shall worship no other god, for the Lord, whose name is *Jealous*, is a *jealous* God" (Exodus 34:14, emphasis mine). Yahweh, the only true and living God, the Creator of the universe, demands the exclusive devotion of his people and is intolerant of any rival.

God requires absolute loyalty, even as a man expects total commitment of his wife. The Mosaic Law made provision for a *jealous* husband.

References to *God's jealousy* are mostly in the context of a marriage relationship with his people. The Bible represents God being wedded to Israel in a covenant relationship. Evan as a husband is jealous over his wife, not wanting another man to woo her, so God is jealous over Israel, not wanting her to wander from her covenant.

Sinful Jealousy

The difference between godly jealousy and sinful jealousy is motive. Every deep emotion turns sinful when it springs from pride and selfishness. Jealousy can be motivated by rivalry or envy which leads to contention and strife. The problem with sinful human beings is that most motives are self-centred with the aim of selfish gain. A God-fearing person, who seeks only the glory of God, will exhibit jealousy for God, but always in a spirit of love and humility.

According to the Christian leaders we interviewed, the largest number of hurts in the ministry, apart from financial struggles, is jealous church leaders and pastors. When church leaders see a young pastor with higher education, doing commendable ministry, they feel threatened and therefore try to stifle the pastor. Opposition from church ministers can be painful. Fellow pastors often see you as competition and not a brother or sister in ministry.

Jealousy springs from many sources: pride, an inferiority complex, an inaccurate view of one's own gifts and calling, lack of contentment, and a rejection of God's sovereign, good, and perfect plan for your life.

The effects of jealousy are serious. Jealousy hinders church growth, creates church division, and causes emotional grief. The fact is that jealousy has no practical benefit. One might say that jealousy and envy are the least practical of vices. They change nothing, make no one happy and lead instead to personal grief and distress.

Overcoming Jealousy

Following are guideposts to avoid jealousy by loving your neighbour.

1. *Know yourself.* Be honest with yourself and humble before God. Recognise and admit your sins of jealousy.
2. *Grow in your knowledge of God.* To know yourself, you must know God intimately through a prayerful reading of Scripture. The more you know God through the Scriptures, the more you will know yourself.
3. *Admit the harm done through jealousy.* Recognise and acknowledge the damage that is done within the church and community through jealousy.

4. *Confess your sin of jealousy.* Pray and confess your sin to God. You cannot hide from God for he knows. Even if you fall into jealousy several times a day, continue to confess your sins with a contrite and broken heart.
5. *Pray for God's blessing upon those of whom you are jealous.* Begin to pray for the welfare of others. When you begin to pray sincerely for their well-being, you will be surprised how God begins to change your heart, filling it with love.
6. *Give thanks to God for those of whom you are jealous.* Thank God for the good which you appreciate in the other. Recognise their gifts and abilities. As you think and pray over the issue, give thanks to God for them.
7. *Tell others about the good you have seen in their lives.* Jesus commanded us to love our enemies. Love can only spring up when we begin to recognise their gifts and abilities that they have received from God. Begin to tell others about the good you have seen in the other.
8. *Begin to compliment those of whom you are jealous.* Counteract thoughts of suspicion of others with words of praise and compliments for those who seem to excel and threaten you.
9. *Learn to accept yourself with all your strengths and weaknesses.* Learn to accept God's loving and sovereign providence. We have nothing to do with the gifts we have received from God, therefore –
10. *Cultivate contentment* for God's gifts to you.

ANGER: THE OPPOSITE OF LOVE

Love builds up, but anger tears down. A Kenyan proverb says: "It is the hyena that howls." Hyenas are scavengers. They roam the countryside in packs to destroy and tear apart. With greed and vicious attacks, they devour and eat. Anger does the same.

Usually, when we think of anger we think of violent outbursts, blowing up with rage and fury. But anger has many lesser manifestations common to everyone. Anger is related to feelings of annoyance, irritation, exasperation, frustration, impatience, indignation, resentment, bitterness, withdrawal, brooding, and hatred.

Ungodly anger is the opposite of love. Love draws you toward the person, but ungodly anger sets you against the person.

Godly and Ungodly Anger

The Bible is filled with warnings against anger. Based on biblical teaching, the ancient Christian church cited anger [wrath] as one of the seven deadly sins. Here are Solomon's proverbs warning against anger:

- Whoever is slow to anger has great understanding, but he who has a hasty temper exalts folly (Proverbs 14:29).
- A hot-tempered man stirs up strife, but he who is slow to anger quiets contention (Proverbs 15:18).
- Whoever is slow to anger is better than the mighty, and he who rules his spirit than he who takes a city (Proverbs 16:32).
- Good sense makes one slow to anger, and it is his glory to overlook an offence (Proverbs 19:11).
- Make no friendship with a man given to anger, nor go with a wrathful man, lest you learn his ways and entangle yourself in a snare (Proverbs 22:24-25).
- Be not quick in your spirit to become angry, for anger lodges in the bosom of fools (Ecclesiastes 7:9).

But it is significant that of the 455 times anger is mentioned in the Old Testament, 375 times it refers to God's anger. In fact, the Bible says "[God] is angry with the wicked every day" (Psalm 7:11, NLT). God in his nature is holy and he is love. Anger is not part of God's nature. Rather, anger is God's response to sins of unrighteousness, ungodliness, and idolatry.

Since Adam and Eve were created in God's image, the human race was endowed with the capacity for anger as well as love. We were made to respond toward injustice and unrighteousness as God does, namely, with righteous anger. Patience in the face of injustice is ungodly. Righteous anger is the appropriate Christian response towards sin.

But since the fall of Adam and Eve, the human emotion of anger usually springs from pride and self with wrong attitudes towards others.

Ungodly anger is the human response when our desires, ambitions, and goals are obstructed or when our dignity is dishonoured. People who are frustrated, upset, disgusted, hostile, bitter, or resentful for one reason or another are exhibiting anger in different forms.

Resolving Ungodly Anger

Christian counsellors estimate that anger is involved in 90 per cent of all those seeking counsel, for anger destroys relationships and peace of mind. How do we handle anger that arises in our hearts and minds?

1. *Be honest with yourself.* Learn to recognise and admit anger when you experience it. Process your anger in a loving, positive, and constructive manner instead of a negative and destructive way.

2. *Never go to bed angry.* Deal with your anger daily and do not allow interpersonal problems to pile up. Be reconciled. Read Matthew 5:21-26.
3. *Learn to control your temper.* If you explode with anger, seek God's help to bring your temper under control. Learn to respond slowly. Count to ten before responding. Speak slowly. Don't raise your voice. Preferably, answer the person only after time to think, pray, and reflect on it.
4. *Learn to forgive.* If you brood over wrongs done to you, a deep-seated bitterness will develop. Learn to forgive and let go. Unconfessed anger will destroy you. Itemise on paper the reasons for your anger. Do you understand the problem correctly or is there another perspective?
5. *Empathise with others.* Listen carefully and try to understand anyone who has offended you. Never respond to an angry person with anger but try to understand the person's predicament from her or his perspective. Walk in the person's shoes.
6. *Never attack others.* Never direct your anger towards others in order to hurt them. Never speak "unwholesome talk" to tear others down (Ephesians 4:29, NIV). Instead of accusing others by saying "you," use "I" statements, such as "I feel frustrated" or "I feel hurt" or "I feel angry."
7. *Love.* Learn to confront with love. Do not remain hurt and angry.
8. *Again and again, learn to forgive* the offender. (See "A Forgiving Spirit" in chapter two.)
9. *Focus on solutions, not problems.* Be solution-oriented, not problem-oriented. Rather than blaming others and brooding, take steps to resolve it.
10. *Reject all self-pity.* Stop thinking of wrongs done to you. Refuse to indulge in self-pity. Count your many blessings. Rejoice in the Lord always. Fill your mind with God's Word. He is the final judge.
11. *Build a healthy self-image.* Lingering anger may indicate an inferiority complex and lack of self-esteem. Be reminded that you are God's child, loved and precious in his sight. Memorize Romans 8:28-39.

THE ATTRIBUTES OF AGAPE LOVE

Leadership is all about people and relationships, and love is at the centre.

Necessity of Love

African Christian leaders declare that the love of people is essential to develop relationships in leadership.

- Ministry is people. It is not money or certificate or a degree. Those coming to ministry need to know that they are dealing with people – some sinful and selfish. Until we know how to deal with people in their context, we cannot succeed (pastor).
- Of first importance, ministers must be people oriented, being involved with people. This means understanding and loving people, being concerned with people. If they are not concerned, if they do not listen to people, their ministry will fail. You cannot rush. You must be a good listener. Think of how they feel, feel with them (Bible school teacher).
- Students in Bible college must be ready to cope with other servants in the ministry. They must fit in with others and have good relationships. If they look down on older pastors and don't respect them, they are in trouble. They must respect them and have fellowship with them. Relationships with people are important (pastor).

How easy is it to work with people? The fact is that people are difficult to lead. People do bring great joy in ministry, but they can also be the leader's worst nightmare. Learning to love these unlovable people is key. As one pastor said, success in ministry comes from "a love for God and love for the people and the ministry. Without love, it is difficult to stay."

Characteristics of Agape Love

Love comes in a variety of expressions: love of friends, parental love of their children, and marital love. The Greek word *agape* is used for the noble love of Christ and which is commanded of all believers. Nowhere does the Bible define *agape*, but it describes *agape* in 1 Corinthians 13, often called the love chapter.

Love Is Patient

J. B. Phillips reads, "[Love] is slow to lose patience." *The Message* says, "Love never gives up." The King James Bible translates it literally, Love "suffereth long." Love has a long temper, the opposite of a short temper. While others fume and fuss, love suffers long.

How important is patience in leadership? According to the Christian leaders we interviewed, patience is *most* important.

- Because of obstacles and problems, you need patience. If you get discouraged easily, you can leave the ministry. Bear with people. Be patient in serving.
- Don't push your ideas on the church. Take your time. Don't push your goals too much because the elders will push you out of the church. As people work with you, they will trust you and will follow you.

Love Is Kind

Patience is the negative side of love. *Agape* bears up under oppression from people and does not strike back. However, one can be patient and yet selfish, neglecting the needs of others. But *agape* is kind in seeking to help others. People don't care much about what you know, but they know if you care about them. Caring for people manifests love.

Love Is Generous

Having stated the two positive traits of love (patience and kindness), Paul mentions the negatives which we have converted into positives. "Love does not envy" or as *The Message* reads: "Love doesn't want what it doesn't have" (1 Corinthians 13:4). *Agape* love is content with what God has entrusted to her. She gives generously instead of envying others.

Love Is Humble

Literally, love does not brag, boast, or show off. J. B. Phillips translates this: "[Love is not] anxious to impress" (13:4). As Proverbs 27:2 says: "Let another praise you, and not your own mouth." Never boast!

Love Is Modest

Literally, "love is not puffed up" as those who puff themselves up to look more important than they really are. As J. B. Phillips reads: "[Love does not] cherish inflated ideas of its own importance" (13:4).

Love Is Courteous

"Love is not . . . rude" (13:4-5, NLT). In other words, love is courteous and has good manners. Love is tactful and considerate of others.

Love Is Unselfish

"Love does not insist on its own way" (13:5) or as *The Message* says: "[Love] isn't always 'me first.'" Unselfish people do not demand their own way.

Love Is Good-Tempered

Love is not easily irritated or provoked to anger. As J. B. Phillips reads: "It is not touchy" (13:4). Love is not easily hurt or offended. Love is even-tempered, calm, and gracious instead of feeling hurt.

Love Is Forgiving

It is easy for one who feels irritated by injustices to store up in the memory a record of those wrongs. But love "keeps no record of wrong" (13:5, NIV). She holds no grudges because she forgives.

Love Is Sincere

Agape is free of pretence or hypocrisy but is sincerely glad when others succeed. She does not gloat over the wrongdoing of others. "Love does not rejoice at wrongdoing, but rejoices with the truth" (13:6).

Conclusion

In Paul's description of *agape* love, he gives four final characteristics: Instead of gossiping about the misdeeds of others like a rumour-monger, *agape* at first covers it up; *agape* believes the best, hoping the report is not true; when *agape* learns the truth, she continues to hope for the best (instead of rejoicing at the worst), and when the misdeeds are finally confirmed, *agape* perseveres in loving the person (13:7).

THE SUPREME MODEL OF AGAPE LOVE

The best way to learn *agape* love is to see it modelled in someone else. But all efforts to imitate God's love are imperfect. Jesus Christ is the only perfect model of God-like love.

Jesus loved people. He loved special friends, like Mary, Martha, and Lazarus (John 11:5). When Lazarus died, we discover that God's incarnate Son wept at the grave of his friend, and the mourners observed, "See how he loved him!" (11:36).

Jesus loved his disciples to the end (John 13:1). In fact, Jesus said, "As the Father has loved me, so have I loved you" (15:9). Amazing love! God-like love! Christ's love for his disciples was a divine love unlike human love. He then added: "Greater love has no one than this, that someone lay down his life for his friends. You are my friends" (15:13-14a). Jesus's supreme example of love is his voluntary death on the cross for his enemies, to grant them forgiveness and eternal life. That is real *agape* love.

But the Gospels speak more often of Christ's love in terms of compassion. On many occasions Jesus felt and showed compassion. The Greek word translated into English as *compassion* means literally, "the inward parts, the entrails." We all have had the experience, when feeling sympathy at the loss of a loved one, of feeling our internal organs being moved. Jesus had this level of deep compassion when identifying with people.

Jesus Had Compassion on People in Need of Help

Jesus was an itinerant preacher and healer, visiting town after town to teach the spiritually hungry and to heal the sick. Matthew observed, "When he [Jesus] saw the crowds, he had *compassion* for them, because they were harassed and helpless, like sheep without a shepherd" (Matthew 9:36, emphasis mine). Instead of being self-absorbed and wishing for some privacy, he was deeply moved – at the gut level – to help the needy crowds surrounding him.

Jesus Felt Compassion for Hungry People

The masses of people were so eager to hear Jesus teach and heal their sick that they stayed with him for several days in the desert. He told his disciples, "I have *compassion* on the crowd because they have been with me now three days and have nothing to eat. And I am unwilling to send them away hungry, lest they faint on the way" (Matthew 15:32, emphasis mine). The disciples had no solution, so Jesus stepped in and fed the 4,000 men besides women and children. He did the same another time, feeding 5,000 men besides women and children. This is compassionate love in action!

Jesus Felt Compassion for the Sick

When Jesus heard of the death of John the Baptist, he invited his disciples to leave their ministry with the crowds and go into a desolate area for thought, reflection, rest, and prayer. But the throngs of people searched for him. No sooner had Jesus and his disciples crossed the Sea of Galilee, they were met with masses of people, the very crowds they sought to avoid. Instead of being frustrated by people demanding Jesus's last ounce of energy, Jesus had compassion on them. He saw people bringing their sick to him for healing. We read Matthew's comment in his Gospel: "When he went ashore he saw a great crowd, and he had *compassion* on them and healed their sick" (Matthew 14:14, emphasis mine). Instead of being obsessed with his own desire for solitude, he had compassion on them and healed the sick.

Jesus Felt Compassion for the Leper

Lepers were ostracised by people who feared contracting this incurable disease, but Jesus, upon seeing a leper begging for help, was "moved with *compassion*" (Mark 1:41,

NLT, emphasis mine) and stretched out his hand to touch this untouchable leper and healed him.

Jesus Felt Compassion on a Widow Whose Only Son Had Died

One day Jesus and his disciples, together with many people, were walking through the town of Nain, when they saw a funeral procession for a young man who had died, the only son of a widow. "And when the Lord saw her, he had *compassion* on her and said to her, 'Do not weep'" (Luke 7:13, emphasis mine). Immediately, he touched the coffin and commanded the son to sit up. He sat up and began to talk How great is Jesus's love for the needy.

Jesus Taught His Followers to Show Compassion on Their Neighbours

In the parable of the "Good Samaritan" Jesus told of a man who was beaten and robbed on his way from Jerusalem to Jericho on a lonely road. Two devout Jews (a priest and a Levite) passed by the hapless victim without extending any help. "But a Samaritan [whom the Jews despised], as he journeyed, came to where he was, and when he saw him, he had *compassion*" (Luke 10:33, emphasis mine). He bound up the wounds and transported him to the nearby inn where they stayed to take care of him, paying the bill himself. Jesus then said: "You go, and do likewise" (10:37).

This is how we are to love our neighbours by showing compassion, even on our enemies and the disreputable. The followers of Christ are to show compassionate love for people even as God our heavenly Father showed compassion on his prodigal son. Upon seeing his son returning home, "his father saw him and was filled with *compassion* for him; he ran to his son, threw his arms around him and kissed him" (Luke 15:20, NIV, emphasis mine). Because of God's love for us, we are commanded to show love for others.

5

Holiness of Christian Leaders

HOLINESS OF THE LORD

Without *humility*, Christian leaders in their pride usurp the glory of God, and thereby invite God's displeasure.

Without *agape* love, Christian leaders fail to reflect God's glorious love, and therefore, cannot be effective Christian leaders.

Without *holiness*, Christian leaders bring reproach on the Lord who said, "Be holy, because I am holy" (1 Peter 1:16, NIV).

Why Is Holiness Important?

Because God Is Holy

The Bible teaches, "The Lord our God is holy" (Psalm 99:9). Holiness refers to the essential character of God. In the throne room of heaven, the seraphs call continually one to another: "Holy, holy, holy is the Lord of hosts; the whole earth is full of his glory!" (Isaiah 6:3). Holiness is important for another reason.

Because God Commands His People to Be Holy

Do you aspire to be a leader? You should never contemplate Christian leadership unless you commit yourself to being holy, living in full obedience to God's commandments. For the Lord commanded his people: "You shall be holy, for I the Lord your God am holy" (Leviticus 19:2).

This moral teaching in the Old Testament is repeated in the New where Peter admonishes us: "As obedient children, do not be conformed to the passions of your former ignorance, but as he who called you is holy, you also be holy in all your conduct, since it is written, 'You shall be holy, for I am holy'" (1 Peter 1:14-16).

Holiness is not a condition for salvation, but it is the fruit of salvation. No evidence of fruit? No assurance of salvation! Holiness of life is evidence of the new birth for the Bible teaches:

> No one who abides in [Christ] keeps on sinning; no one who keeps on sinning has either seen him or known him. Little children, let no one deceive you. Whoever practices righteousness is righteous, as he is righteous. Whoever makes a practice of sinning is of the devil, for the devil has been sinning from the beginning . . . No one born of God makes a practice of sinning, for God's seed abides in him, and he cannot keep on sinning because he has been born of God (1 John 3:6-9).

What Is Holiness?

The concept of holiness is derived from the Hebrew Old Testament word, *qadash*, which contains two ideas.

Apartness or Separateness

God is holy in the sense that he is distinct from and separate from all creation. Expressing this thought, God says: "I am God and not a man, the Holy One in your midst" (Hosea 11:9). God is eternally and fundamentally set apart from his creation. But God's holiness is more often referring to his moral character.

Righteous Character

Holiness is separation from all that is morally unclean or evil. To be holy is to be morally righteous, separated from sin and consecrated to God.

God's holiness in this respect is manifest in his separation from all that is unclean and impure. God is holy in the sense that he is totally righteousness. Christian leaders above all others must strive to be holy lest they fall under God's judgment.

What Is the Standard of Holiness?

The fundamental basis for the divine standard of holiness is the character of God. The commandments in Scripture are not arbitrary *dos and don'ts*. All the divine commandments which bind Christians today are rooted in the very character of God. The first man and woman were made in the image of God, reflecting his holiness.

The biblical summary of God's righteous standards is the Ten Commandments (Exodus 20) and was deepened by Jesus (Matthew 5–7).

The first commandments, pertaining to our relationship with God, call on God's covenant people to acknowledge the majestic and singular holiness of the Lord, and to offer him absolute and total allegiance and worship.

The last commandments, pertaining to our relationships with one another (not to murder, commit adultery, steal, lie, and covet), are grounded in God's holy love. Because God is love, those made in his image are commanded to love one another. "For the whole law is fulfilled in one word: 'You shall love your neighbour as yourself'" (Galatians 5:14).

Our Lord made the astonishing statement: "You therefore must be perfect, as your heavenly Father is perfect" (Matthew 5:48). Is this really possible? Can a Christian leader live a holy life even as God is holy? The Bible clearly states that this should be the goal for all Christians and especially for Christian leaders. Paul declares that overseers "must be above reproach" (1 Timothy 3:2). This is possible through the power of the Holy Spirit as we utilize the means of grace.

INTEGRITY

Integrity is at the heart of what it means to be holy, and it is essential for Christian leadership. To be a leader one must have followers. To have followers they must have confidence in their leader. To have confidence in the leadership requires integrity of the leader.

What Is Integrity?

Synonyms for integrity include honesty, truthfulness, veracity, reliability, and uprightness. The opposite of integrity is dishonesty. A more basic meaning of integrity can be traced to the Latin word *integritas,* meaning soundness, whole, complete, intact, and perfect – perfect in the sense of being pure, unmixed, unadulterated, complete, and unblemished.

Therefore, to understand integrity one must go beyond the meaning of honesty. A person of integrity is not a *moral chameleon*, changing to accommodate the popular view of the moment. Neither are persons of integrity *opportunists* whose primary goal is personal gain who change and adapt to accommodate others for one's own personal advantage. Neither are persons of integrity *hypocrites*, pretending to be what they are not.

In brief, persons of integrity are honest, truthful, reliable, and upright and whose whole beings are simple, whole, undivided, and perfect. Their words are always truthful and consistent. Their values and principles are always consistent with God's holy standard. Their moral character is always upright. They are the same in public as in private, the same inwardly and outwardly, and the same with family and strangers.

Why Is Integrity So Important?

Moral integrity for Christian leaders is essential for two major reasons: God is perfect in his integrity and commands Christian leaders to have integrity.

God's Perfect Integrity

God is always truthful and honest in what he says as the Scriptures teach: "The Glory of Israel will not lie" (1 Samuel 15:29). In fact, "it is impossible for God to lie" (Hebrews 6:18). Whereas Satan is "a liar and the father of lies" who "speaks out of his own character" (John 8:44), it is contrary to God's nature to lie. Although God is almighty and can do all things, he *cannot* lie because he cannot go contrary to his own nature.

God is always faithful in keeping his promises. What he says, he will do. The faithfulness of God is prominent throughout Scripture. Moses says: "Know therefore that the Lord your God is God, *the faithful* God who keeps covenant and steadfast love with those who love him" (Deuteronomy 7:9, emphasis mine). David sings: "*Your faithfulness* [extends] to the clouds" (Psalm 36:5, emphasis mine). The prophets proclaim: "Great is *your faithfulness*" (Lamentations 3:23, emphasis mine).

Not only is God honest, truthful, upright, and faithful, he is genuinely so. His very Being is pure and unadulterated. He is not a chameleon which changes its colour and markings to gain advantage. God does not and cannot change. God is not hypocritical, saying one thing today and another thing tomorrow. As the Westminster shorter catechism states: "God is a Spirit, infinite, eternal, and *unchangeable, in his being, wisdom, power, holiness, justice, goodness, and truth*" (emphasis mine).

Integrity of Christian Leaders

Christian leaders must continually grow into the likeness of their heavenly Father even as all Christians are commanded "to put on the new self, created after the likeness of God in true righteousness and holiness" (Ephesians 4:24). Christian leaders are not perfect. They make mistakes and may sin against God and before others. But they should be growing in the Lord, growing in their likeness to the Lord.

Paul admonished a young church leader: "Show yourself in all respects to be *a model of good works*, and in your teaching *show integrity*, dignity, and sound speech that cannot be condemned" (Titus 2:7-8, emphasis mine). Some preachers are insincere in their preaching. They preach with ulterior motives. They seek personal gain and profit through their gospel of prosperity. They preach what they do not practice. It is incumbent for all Christian leaders to conduct themselves with absolute integrity. Always remember what David knew 3,000 years ago: "I know, my

God, that you test the heart and are *pleased with integrity*" (1 Chronicles 29:17, NIV, emphasis mine).

Integrity in character means telling the truth, never lying. Christian leaders must always be honest, truthful, reliable, and upright.

Integrity in character includes faithfulness. God expects his servants to be faithful, even as he is faithful. "It is required that those who have been given a trust must prove *faithful*" (1 Corinthians 4:2, NIV, emphasis mine). Faithfulness is the one requirement for Christian service. Success measured by this world includes position, power, and prestige. But God will never reward for such achievements. He will reward for *faithfulness*.

A Christian leader must also be real, genuinely real. No amount of talking will convince anyone if you are not genuine in your profession. After some time, the lay people will see through your insincerity. They will look beyond your charismatic character and preaching and see through you. Chameleons try to deceive others but in time people will see your lack of integrity.

PURITY

One of the greatest reasons for failing in ministry is impurity. After years of observation and reflection, I have concluded that the three basic reasons why people fail in ministry are: lust of the flesh (immorality, impurity), lust of the eyes (greed, stealing, and misappropriation of funds), and the pride of life (pride – struggles for power, position, and prestige). See 1 John 2:16.

To avoid crashing in ministry, Paul advised Timothy: "Keep yourself *pure*" (1 Timothy 5:22, emphasis mine). Every Christian leader who is "holy to the Lord" must take concrete steps to keep pure to please the holy God and be effective in ministry.

Young leaders, fresh out of training, are often faced with rejection by the elders because of their youth and lack of experience. Paul had good advice for young Timothy: "Let no one despise you for your youth, *but set the believers an example* in speech, in conduct, in love, in faith, *in purity*" (1 Timothy 4:12, emphasis mine).

Meaning of Purity

We read of the New Jerusalem having streets of "pure gold" and a river flowing with pure water "bright as crystal" (Revelation 21:18; 22:1). That is, the water is not polluted with dirt, and the gold is not alloyed with any other mineral.

In the spiritual realm purity refers to the absence of defilement from sin. To live a pure life is to live a morally chaste, clean life in thought, word, and deed.

When speaking of purity of life, the Bible usually refers to a life free from sexual impurity.

The seventh commandment of the Decalogue is terse: "You shall not commit adultery" (Exodus 20:14). Adultery refers to sexual intercourse between a married person and someone who is not their spouse. This commandment is intended to protect the marriage bond between husband and wife.

Marital faithfulness is obligatory. Since marriage and family are foundational for society, protecting that marital bond is important. "He who commits adultery lacks sense; he who does it destroys himself" (Proverbs 6:32).

But sexual purity reaches beyond the bounds of marriage. Sexual relationships between members of the same sex are forbidden in both the Old Testament and New Testament (Leviticus 18:22; 20:13; Jude 7). Fornication, the sexual intercourse between unmarried persons, is likewise forbidden. The Bible warns: "*Flee from sexual immorality*. All other sins a person commits are outside the body, but whoever sins sexually sins against their own body" (1 Corinthians 6:18, NIV, emphasis mine). Most cultures today are saturated with lustful temptations through music, television, movies, and the internet.

Jesus deepens the spiritual meaning of the Ten Commandments. He went beyond the literal letter of the law when he taught the following:

> You know the next commandment pretty well, too: "Don't go to bed with another's spouse." But don't think you've preserved your virtue simply by staying out of bed. Your *heart* can be corrupted by lust even quicker than your *body*. Those ogling looks you think nobody notices – they also corrupt (Matthew 5:27-28, MSG).

Dangers of Sexual Addiction

The sin of lusting after another can become addictive. Lust becomes attached to fantasies which, if left uncontrolled, become obsessions which are addictions. Beware!

In our day of the internet a grave danger is pornography. It can easily be found on the web. In the secrecy of the home or church office it can be viewed. Pornography is so dangerous that many a Christian leader has fallen into grave sin, marriages have been destroyed, and God's name has been reproached. Pornography is a fire which will destroy the soul.

Several warning signs may point to a Christian leader's struggle with sexual addiction, including trouble in one's marriage, counselling a person at strange times or in secretive places, spending a lot of time alone, use of sexual humour, or visiting questionable places.

Advice on How to Avoid Sexual Immorality

1. *Be honest with yourself.* Admit the problem. Don't deny it.
2. *Recognise that you are in a spiritual battle.* Your old, carnal nature is drawn to sensual pleasure that is contrary to God's will.
3. *Repent, confess, and draw near to God through prayer and the meditation on God's Word.* Nothing strengthens the inner person to resist sin like the Word of God with the empowering of the Spirit.
4. *Stop fantasizing.* This may not be easy. Just as drug addicts experience struggles and withdrawal symptoms, people who have conditioned themselves to respond with sexual fantasies when aroused by certain sights, times, or smells, will struggle.
5. *Stop feeding fantasies.* Starve your lustful desires. Don't feed them. Stop listening to music with suggestive lyrics. Stop completely. Stop watching TV programmes with sexual innuendos. Stop completely!
6. *Seek a prayer partner* with whom you can share and to whom you are accountable. Do everything necessary to defeat this demon.

HONESTY

One of the three greatest temptations for Christian leaders is dishonesty. Christian leaders are particularly vulnerable to dishonesty for several reasons. First, pastors and elders handle the money contributed in church. They may collude and share some of the contributions for personal needs. Excuses are many. Pastors are not paid well, and besides, they may initially only intend to borrow it. Second, there may be lack of transparency and accountability. Money is counted behind closed doors, sometimes by one person only. Third, Christian leaders sometimes mix their own money with the money belonging to the church and confusion arises. While the initial purpose is innocent, the lack of accountability creates a problem.

Biblical Teaching on Dishonesty

The eighth commandment is straightforward: "You shall not steal." Dishonesty includes lying, cheating, and stealing. Stealing is taking anything that belongs to another. It is misappropriation of funds. In contrast honesty includes integrity, sincerity, and truthfulness.

All sins grow in poisoned clusters. No doubt anyone who steals has first coveted those things. To cover over stealing, there is lying and deceit. To steal is to break the law of loving your neighbour as yourself. You cannot break one commandment without breaking several others together.

Dishonesty is practiced in a variety of ways including the taking of money from church funds. One may think, "I need this for transport in ministry," or "I was not paid my salary this month and I need to buy food."

A Christian leader may only want to borrow the money with full intentions of repaying it. The sin is not borrowing money but doing this without official permission and proper accountability.

A less obvious form of stealing is laziness – not working as the employer expects. A church secretary, becoming busy only when the supervisor comes around, is being unfaithful. Pastors are either the busiest people in the parish, on-duty 24 hours seven days a week, or they are potentially the laziest people without any supervisor to check their faithfulness.

Shoplifting (stealing goods from stores), cheating on paying taxes, being careless with something that is borrowed, or failing to return what is borrowed are other forms of stealing. Jumping the queue (line) in the post office may seem innocent, but depriving someone else of his or her rightful place is a form of stealing. There are scores of ways to cheat and take from others what does not rightfully belong to you. We do not love our neighbour as ourselves when we steal.

A Biblical View of Wealth

It is true that the Old Testament generally sees wealth as a blessing given by God,[7] but it also warns of the dangers of wealth.[8] "Better is a little with the fear of the Lord than great treasure and trouble with it" (Proverbs 15:16). Solomon offered the best advice: "Give me neither poverty nor riches; feed me with the food that is needful for me, lest I be full and deny you and say, 'Who is the Lord?' or lest I be poor and steal and profane the name of my God" (Proverbs 30:8-9).

Jesus spoke a great deal about riches and always negatively. He stated bluntly: "You cannot serve God and money" (Matthew 6:24). He warned: "Take care, and be on your guard against all covetousness, for one's life does not consist in the abundance of one's possessions" (Luke 12:15). Jesus taught: "Where your treasure is, there your heart will be also" (Matthew 6:21).

Practical Advice for Christian Leaders

This is a very practical problem for those in ministry. We all need food, housing, medical care, and other necessities. Poverty is a real curse which can make people feel helpless and lose their self-esteem.

On the other hand, money has been a problem for Christian leaders from the beginning of the church. Paul's counsel to Timothy and the early churches he shepherded stands for all time:

> There is *great gain in godliness with contentment*, for we brought nothing into the world, and we cannot take anything out of the world. But if we have food and clothing, with these we will be content. But *those who desire to be rich fall into temptation*, into a snare, into many senseless and harmful desires that plunge people into ruin and destruction. *For the love of money is a root of all kinds of evils*. It is through this craving that some have wandered away from the faith (1 Timothy 6:6-10, emphasis mine).

Following is some advice to which you may add additional thoughts:

1. *Develop a spirit of contentment*. Life lived with dissatisfaction and discontentment is not worth living. Focus on God, spouse, children, blessings, and the promises of God. Say "no" to covetousness.
2. *Grow in your relationship with God*. Find your joy in him. Learn to trust him. Read Philippians 4:11-13 for Paul's experience.
3. *Distinguish between Needs and Wants*. God promises to provide all our needs, but not our wants (Philippians 4:19).

THE PURE IN HEART

"Blessed are the pure in heart, for they shall see God" (Matthew 5:8). Nothing is more important in life than your *heart*. The heart is where everything begins. Whenever you learn of shocking behaviour by someone, whether it is sexual immorality or theft or any other moral defect, always remember this – it was preceded by thoughts and desires that were entertained and nurtured in the heart for some time.

Biblical Meaning of the Heart

The Old Testament Hebrew word *leb* is translated as "heart" and used most of the time in a figurative sense for the innermost part of a person. This is the *inner* self as opposed to the *outer* self. The heart is the seat of the mind, will, and emotions. The *mind* (heart) remembers, considers, thinks, and reflects. The *emotions* (heart) feel joy and gladness, sorrow, and vexation. The *will* (heart) resolves, decides, and inclines to do things.

The New Testament word for "heart" is the Greek word *kardia* and reflects the Old Testament usage, referring to the inner self.

Biblical Importance of the Heart

An insightful African proverb states: "As the wound inflames the finger, so a thought can inflame the mind." Careful attention must be given to the care of the mind for an inflamed mind (heart) leads to bad outcomes.

The purity or impurity of external actions reflects the purity or impurity of the heart. Everything of human importance begins in the heart. Why is this true?

All Sin Comes from the Heart

Jesus taught that all sin comes from the heart. The Pharisees were concerned with external purity – washing hands, cups, pots, and copper vessels. They were concerned with ceremonial cleansing. But Jesus confronted the Jews because they were concerned only with external cleansing while neglecting inner purity, saying:

> What comes out of a person is what defiles him. *For from within, out of the heart of man, come* evil thoughts, sexual immorality, theft, murder, adultery, coveting, wickedness, deceit, sensuality, envy, slander, pride, foolishness. All these things come from within, and they defile a person (Mark 7:20-23, emphasis mine).

Examine the list of sins mentioned above by Jesus. They include *everything* that we have been discussing in this book. Godly character comes from a pure heart and ungodly character from an impure heart. The primary way to deal with ungodly character is to deal with the heart.

Whatever Is Stored in the Heart Is Revealed Outwardly

Jesus taught that the type of tree is known by its fruit, then spoke of the importance of the heart: "The good person out of the good treasure of his heart produces good, and the evil person out of his evil treasure produces evil, *for out of the abundance of the heart his mouth speaks*" (Luke 6:45, emphasis mine).

Biblical Truth of Guarding the Heart

The main avenue of storing thoughts in the heart is through the eye and ear gates. Through the eyes and ears we build up treasures in the heart that will become manifest through the mouth speaking and the hands and feet doing.

The secret of having a pure heart is to guard it: Solomon wrote: "Above all else, guard your heart, for everything you do flows from it" (Proverbs 4:23, NIV).

- *Above all else:* Nothing is more important in life than to do this.
- *Guard your heart:* The Christian leader is in a spiritual battle. Satan seeks your downfall. A military stance of guarding is necessary to prevent defeat.
- *For everything you do flows from it:* The kind of life you will live springs up from the heart. What you feed your mind shapes your words and conduct.

This is a major challenge in our fallen world. What kind of music do you listen to? What kind of TV do you watch? What do you read on the internet? Lust permeates our modern-day cultures in popular songs, advertisements, movies, internet, books, and magazines.

Decisions need to be made all the time of what to watch and what to listen to. How do you decide? Here are several questions to consider, based on the following Scriptures: 1 Corinthians 6:12; 8:13; 10:31; Romans 12:2.

- Is it helpful – does it build you up spiritually and mentally?
- Does it bring you under its power – are you becoming enslaved?
- Does it hurt others – cause them to stumble and fall?
- Is God glorified? What would Jesus do? Would he listen to this, watch this, go here, do that? This is a major issue.

By watching and listening to garbage in our degenerate age, Christians lose their sensitivity to the spiritual standards of morality. Like a frog in a kettle of water, without knowing that the water is getting hotter to a boiling point, the Christian's conscience is destroyed, and God's servant is ruined.

Not only must the heart *be guarded from temptations* coming through the eye and ear gates, the heart must also *be filled with God's thoughts*. "Do not be conformed to this world, but be *transformed by the renewal of your mind*" (Romans 12:2, emphasis mine). This can only happen through the discipline of meditating on God's Word and in prayer.

6

Attributes of Christian Leaders

Not only should Christian leaders have *character* that is "beyond reproach," they should have *competence* in the field of leadership. While Christian leaders may fail because of faulty character, many godly Christian leaders fail to live up to their potential because they do not know the principles of good management.

The first part of this book dealt with *character* while the latter part of this book, beginning with chapter 6, is devoted to competence of leaders.

THE NATURE OF CHRISTIAN LEADERSHIP

If you want to lead, you need to know the nature of Christian leadership.

Who Can Be Called a Leader?

Many consider themselves leaders because they hold the *position* of leadership, but many occupy the seat of leadership without being a leader.

Certain people are born leaders with a commanding personality, but that natural gift does not guarantee successful leadership. Actual leaders are those who have followers, those who influence others to follow them. Genuine leaders have ability to make things happen because of their dynamic personality and leadership traits.

In reality there are many styles of leadership, but all leaders must have followers who believe in them and are influenced by them. Every leader inspires and motivates his or her followers to do things together to accomplish great things and achieve significant goals. A leader makes things happen.

What Is the Difference Between a Leader and a *Christian* Leader?

A Christian leader shares many of the qualities of a natural leader. A leader is a visionary leading the way. A leader is inspirational and motivational with followers and is effective as a change agent.

The essential distinction between a natural leader and a Christian leader is his or her relationship with God in Christ. Christian leaders see themselves as *under*-shepherds, serving under the direction of Christ and doing God's will. Christian leaders are servant-leaders, serving God pre-eminently and others secondarily and not themselves.

All too often Christian leaders follow the pattern of the world. God condemned Israel's shepherd-leaders for feeding themselves instead of the sheep. Good shepherds feed the sheep, strengthen the weak, heal the sick, bind up the injured, and look for the lost sheep which go astray. Instead of profiting selfishly from their leadership position as so many do, they should care for the sheep and diligently follow God's will (Ezekiel 34:1-4).

What Is the Leader's Relationship with Her or His Followers?

Leaders should see themselves as a *team* leader and not a *boss* leader. A leader is blessed to have members on his or her team with differing gifts. A leader understands that no one, not even the leader, has all the gifts necessary to do the job; that no one is a leader without the team uniting and sharing both responsibilities and recognition. Team members participate in the work using their unique gifts and receiving recognition for their work.

This requires a *team spirit.* Developing a team spirit is the responsibility of the team leader. A positive spirit is essential. No pessimist can unite a team. Welding a team together so that they are enthusiastic, motivated, and energized toward achieving a common goal is the leader's great challenge.

What Part Does Culture Play in Shaping Leadership?

As we have seen in chapter 3, a *team leader* does not fit naturally in every cultural tradition of African peoples. Some communities were more participatory and less authoritarian in leadership. If a leader behaved like a big man in those communities, the people would not respect him.

However, the big-man mentality – common among leaders today – was prevalent in the past among many communities. The leader was the final authority. It is true that the chief worked with the council of elders. But in the end the chief's decision was personal. Though the chief's decisions were formed by consultations, the decision was not necessarily the will of the majority. Once made, no one dared to challenge the chief's decision.

This authoritarian way of leadership is inherent within human sinful nature. The reality is that the big-man culture persists today throughout the world and influences both society and the church leadership.

We have all observed that before being chosen as a church leader, many are people of integrity. But after the election and after some years leaders become corrupt and assert their privileged position. It has been said that it is in all of us. That consciously or unconsciously, we often become the bullies we have hated. In campaigns, leaders may point to the failures of others, but after winning the election those same leaders often become like the very people they condemned.

The faithful Christian leader, however, rises above the norm and determines with God's help to be a *servant-leader*, under the authority of Jesus Christ and serving as a faithful shepherd for the welfare of the sheep.

MARKS OF AN EFFECTIVE LEADER

The Bible says: "The mark of a good leader is loyal followers" (Proverbs 14:28, MSG). Today the experts in management agree. But what can be found in leaders that causes their followers to be so loyal?

Marks of a Leader in African Tradition

Following is a composite of the marks of a traditional African leader taken from many communities.

- *Age:* Traditionally, wisdom was learned in the University of Experience. The older one was, the wiser he became. Young people could never imagine doing anything without first seeking advice from the elders who were held in deep respect and fear.
- *Wisdom:* The leader was expected to understand people and their situations and how to tackle their problems. It was not simply old age that brought you respect but your wisdom and knowledge, and what you have been able to do to prove yourself.
- *Wealth:* Traditionally, wealth gave power to elders. A leader was expected to work hard and not be lazy so that he could accumulate cattle and goats and become wealthy.
- *Generosity:* Wealth caused people to respect you because you were able to provide food for the hungry and give a cow for the council of elders to eat. In a sense, "You bought your way to the top of leadership." Generosity from your wealth was essential.
- *Many wives and children:* The more wives and children, the more respect an elder received.

- *Courageous:* Leaders did not fear anything. The leader was strong to fight. He could never be weak.
- *Articulate communicator:* The leader was an articulate speaker at public gatherings. He was "chairman" of the council. He guided and controlled the discussion.
- *Supernatural powers:* In some communities the people recognised a potential leader because he was untouchable with protection from witchcraft. He was known as a "mysterious man," such as a rainmaker, a prophet, or someone with mystical powers.
- *An exemplary life:* The leader was to be an example for others.
- *Uniting the community:* The leader was capable of handling all kinds of disputes, such as family struggles and inter-clan conflicts.

Marks of an Effective Christian Leader

Following are the responses of African Christian leaders we interviewed:

Personality Characteristics

- *A People Person:* Since leadership is relational with followers, being a people-person is foundational. A loner who moves forward all alone can have no followers; hence, he is no leader.
- *Visionary:* A leader must see ahead and have a vision where he wants to lead the people. Once the leader and his team embrace a vision with goals for the future, the leader maintains that focus.
- *Commands Respect:* People desire a strong leader who is fully assured, confident, and knowledgeable. His followers respect him.
- *Strength with Flexibility:* Courage and strength enable a leader to make decisions, but flexibility, the ability to change and adapt, is also essential. While decisions must be made wisely, once made, vacillation and hesitation must never occur.
- *Dispensable:* An effective leader recognises that his leadership is not unending, that he really is dispensable in God's timing.
- *Wisdom and Knowledge:* Decision making requires discernment and this comes from maturity and years of experience. Knowledge is knowing the facts; wisdom combines good understanding with good judgment. A leader needs both knowledge and wisdom.
- *Persuasive Speaker:* A leader must master communication skills.
- *Ever Learning:* He needs to know he has much more to learn.

Moral Character

- *A Model to Follow:* In every dimension of life, he is a model.
- *Humble:* He accepts and admits mistakes. He is willing to say, "I am sorry." He is willing to change his ways when rebuked.
- *Patient:* Many quit, but an effective leader perseveres.
- *Fair-Minded:* Prejudice and unfair treatment destroy team spirit.
- *Self-Sacrificial:* A genuine leader sacrifices himself for the good.
- *Grateful:* A leader should appreciate anything good received from people. Express thanks and gratitude towards others.
- *Humorous:* He should not take himself too seriously and be able to laugh at himself. Be jovial and encouraging – remain positive.
- *Loyal:* As a father figure to his team, he should defend and protect them, making them feel secure from attack.
- *Faithful:* Leaders are required to carry out responsibilities faithfully and protect the resources. Integrity is essential.

MISTAKES OF CHRISTIAN LEADERS

Following are comments derived both from African Christian leaders who shared their wealth of experience and observation, and from other Christian leaders who have written about mistakes of leaders. These are short, pithy statements that have been developed elsewhere in this book.

1. *Spiritual insensitivity:* Due to busyness or delinquency, Christian leaders often lapse in their spiritual disciplines of prayer and meditation on God's Word. This leads to insensitivity to the Holy Spirit in leading them.
2. *Pride:* The greatest mistake is formed in the mind. People think they are leaders because they are the best ones to lead. They feel they know it all. They will not listen to others because they think, "I know it because I am the leader." In African culture the leader is always right, and this tradition has flowed into the church today.
3. *Living in sin:* Some leaders live in sin and feel comfortable with it. They follow their evil ways while hiding it from people. One leader told me: "Hiding sin has killed the church in Africa today."
4. *Nepotism:* Nepotism is appointing people to positions because they are from your own family, clan, tribe, or circle of friends even though they do not qualify. A leader must resist such enormous pressure and choose to do the right thing.

An effective leader will always choose the best qualified personnel who can move the ministry toward accomplishing the goals. Doing this will redound to the leader's own benefit.

5. *Favouritism:* The leader will naturally appreciate some team members more than others, either because of their personality, contribution, or some relationship. But leaders make divisive mistakes whenever they favour one person over the other. Tribalism and clannism are deadly mistakes. Favouritism can take another form when the leader works with only a few of the elders instead of all the elders and the whole congregation, keeping the others in the dark. The end result will be division.
6. *Overcommitment:* A leader who becomes overly busy because of accepting too many responsibilities will not be able to do anything well. You must determine before the Lord what your focus should be – that goal which you desire under God to fulfil and do well.
7. *Indecisiveness:* Weak leaders find difficulty making decisions and acting upon those decisions. They listen to different viewpoints and then vacillate. They are swayed one way by some and another way by others. Leaders should consult and they must be wise. They should take time in all decision-making. But after investigation, thought, and prayer, a decision must be made, and that decision must be firmly kept without wavering.
8. *Inadequate training:* Education is no substitute for the gift of leadership. But gifted leadership without training will leave the person bereft and unable to fulfil full potential. Some church leaders do not value education, but they are mistaken. A solid, basic education is foundational. Reading books, attending seminars, and taking courses can help leaders keep growing and remain refreshed with new ideas.
9. *Failure to plan:* Because of lack of training and understanding, many leaders just deal with things as they come. Churches fail to grow when their leaders do not think and plan for the future.
10. *Unprepared successor:* Assuming that you will be the president, bishop, chairman, or principal for life is the sign of a failed leader. No leader is successful if he or she does not prepare a successor. Organisations fail when the leader does not prepare a successor.
11. *Failure to delegate:* Many leaders try to do everything themselves. Such leaders will be overcome with work. They fail to develop others because they fear losing

their own position to someone better than themselves. Such an approach is short-sighted and doomed to failure.

12. *Neglect of teaching:* Many pastors fail to provide systematic teaching from the Scriptures. Each Sunday they jump from one topic to another. They have no plan to teach the whole counsel of the Word of God.
13. *Slandering others:* Gossiping about the failures of others or slandering other members on your ministry team can only bring division and dissension. An effective leader knows how to control her or his tongue.
14. *Breaking confidentiality:* Nothing destroys confidence in the leader more than the breaking of confidentiality. Team members must be assured that whatever they confide with the leader will remain confidential. This is one of the laws of the Medes and the Persians – *never to be broken.*
15. *Unwise discipline:* Leaders create all kinds of problems when they exercise discipline on team members hastily without adequate research and understanding of the situation.
16. *Hasty actions:* The unwise leader will rush into decisions without patience and wise counsel, pushing ahead without the consensus or support of the elders and people. Messy situations are the result.

You can also learn of leadership mistakes from the Book of Proverbs such as: laziness, lack of knowledge and wisdom, disregarding advice, rash speaking, slander and gossip, lack of self-control, partiality, giving up, and being stingy.

THE LEADER AS CHANGE AGENT

Anyone worthy of being called a leader is a *change agent.* In this world everything becomes old or dirty and needs to be changed—made new. Christian leaders, who serve as God's under-shepherds, must facilitate change for God's glory and the building of his kingdom.

Resistance to Change

Most people are conservative and resist change. Change is difficult, but if a church or ministry organisation does not change over time, it becomes stagnant and begins the process of dying. Change is difficult but inevitable. As Heraclitus, the ancient Greek philosopher once said, "Nothing is permanent except change."

Jesus never changes and God's truth never changes, but everything else changes over time.

All organisations and organisms tend to go through certain cycles: birth, infancy, childhood, adolescence, adulthood, middle age, greying years, old age, and death. In the early stages an organisation has vibrant energy and ability to change, but as time passes it becomes rigid and resistant to change. Eventually, it fades away and dies.

People object to change by saying "That's impossible," or "We don't do things that way around here," or "We tried something like that before and it didn't work," or "I wish it were that easy." For these reasons a leader must be patient and wise whenever implementing change.

Qualities of a Change Agent

The leader as a change-agent needs three characteristics: *creativity* to explore what changes are needed, *courage* to bring about change, and *wisdom* to know how to lead in change.

Creativity

Creativity is the creation of a new idea, but creativity must be followed by innovation which puts creative ideas into action. Ideally, the leader is a creative person for he or she must lead in bringing about change. But creative ideas also come from the grassroots. The role of the leader is to stimulate his or her team members to think beyond the status quo.

Change for change's sake is futile. But change to improve and grow is a sign of youthful vigour. Leaders with their teams should be asking many questions: "How can we in our church, institution, or ministry organisation be more faithful and pleasing to God?" "What new problems or conditions are arising?" "What changes would help us minister better in these changing conditions?" Prayerfully read the Scripture, talk to people, think, and imagine creatively about the changes that might make a difference!

Courage

Timid leaders are afraid of the negative consequences of change. They fear making decisions because of possible ramifications.

Courage for a Christian comes through trust in God's ability to guide and help. It comes through meditating on Scriptures and prayerfully waiting on God for guidance just as Joshua was taught (Joshua 1:6-8).

Wisdom

A Kenyan proverb says: "Wisdom outweighs strength." Great wisdom is needed to avoid mistakes. Following are some basic principles.

1. *Go slowly.* No principle is more African than this. A Swahili proverb says: "Hurry, hurry brings no blessing." The Kamba say: "Slowly, slowly is the way to go."

   No principle is more important. *Never* make or suggest changes during the first year of ministry. Trust must first be earned before venturing into the difficult task of suggesting change. Move slowly.

2. *Engage in prayer, reflection, and sharing.* If Christ is the Lord of the church, then his people must be in thoughtful prayer and reflection to determine God's will. Instead of forcing one's will, let God lead the way.

3. *Enlist team members in decisions.* Change comes more easily when the group has participated in the decision-making process. Resistance arises from surprise announcements. Some African leaders may not feel a need to consult. As one person said: "In my culture the leader does not need to seek the opinion of his people in order to make decisions." That may be a cultural tradition when people were not educated, but in our modern societies of Africa today failure to seek the opinion of people is dangerous.

   A wise African Christian leader commented: "I would say, it is very important to seek consensus. If a leader makes a decision without consulting, if the project fails, he is considered a failure. But if the decision is made by consensus, leaders are not considered failures."

4. *Provide motivation for change.*
   - Inspire with a vision or dream of what could be accomplished.
   - Talk of rewards and benefits that will flow from the change.
   - Communicate freely, frequently, and effectively so that everyone is brought together with the excitement of the future prospect.
   - Be transparent and accountable to your team so that they will gain trust in you as the leader.
   - Be sincere and genuine, humble, and willing to admit mistakes, weaknesses, and limitations.
   - Gain credibility by showing confidence and knowledge.
   - Help people see how their problems will be resolved by change.
   - Receive and utilize suggestions coming from the people.

NEHEMIAH: A MODEL LEADER

A Christian leader relies on God totally but accepts full responsibility. This principle of Christian leadership and more can be found in the book of Nehemiah as he led the Jews to rebuild Jerusalem after the captivity.

The events of Nehemiah occurred after the destruction of Jerusalem in 587 BC when Nebuchadnezzar took thousands of Jews into captivity. After the seventy-year Babylonian captivity, Cyrus, the Persian king, issued an edict permitting the return of the Jews to their home country. Ezra records the first return of 49,897 Jews under Zerubbabel in 538 BC. The exiles rebuilt the altar and offered sacrifices. Under the prophetic ministry of Haggai and Zechariah the temple was completed in 515 BC.

Nehemiah's account begins in 445 BC when he learned of the frightful conditions of the Jewish exiles who had returned to Jerusalem. Without a wall built around the city of Jerusalem, the people were under continual harassment by their enemies. The account of Nehemiah's response to this dismal report from Jerusalem displays a model of leadership from which every Christian leader should learn.

Following are the attributes of leadership in the life of Nehemiah.

1. *Nehemiah manifested an unselfish concern for God's people.* Nehemiah served in an elevated and comfortable position as the cupbearer to King Artaxerxes I of Persia. But instead of striving to keep his noble position with its luxuries, he showed unselfish concern for his people. Unlike Nehemiah, many Christian leaders use their position for greedy gain and selfish interests. The Bible warns against this (1 Peter 5:2).
2. *Nehemiah identified with his people.* Effective leaders identify with the people they lead. They do not look down on the people or distance themselves from them. Nehemiah identified himself with the Jews whose sin led to the captivity before he was born. "I now pray . . . confessing the sins of the people of Israel, which we have sinned against you. Even I and my father's house have sinned. We have acted very corruptly . . ." (Nehemiah 1:6-7, emphasis mine). An effective leader thinks in terms of "we and us", not "you and me."
3. *Nehemiah was a student of God's Word and taught it to the people.* Nehemiah exemplifies an effective Christian leader who was filled with the Word of God as evidenced by his prayers. He also ensured the Jews were instructed in the Word of God. He arranged for the people to hear the Word of God read for three hours. His decisions were informed by God's Word.

4. *Nehemiah depended on God in prayer.* Nehemiah was a man of prayer. Nine prayers are recorded in his memoirs. He approached God with reverence and in humility confessed his sins. On the basis of the promises in Scripture he interceded on behalf of his people. He prayed "without ceasing" as evidenced by his frequent prayers in the midst of his ministry.

5. *Nehemiah had a personal relationship with God.* Prayer can be formal and nominal. Christian leaders often lead in prayer as a custom. But Nehemiah's prayers indicate an intimate knowledge of God. He *knew* God.

6. *Nehemiah had courageous faith.* After praying and reflecting on the report of Jerusalem's plight for four months, he courageously approached the king with a huge request. When the wealthy Jews in Jerusalem oppressed the poor, he erupted in righteous indignation against the influential wealthy class. Leaders cannot succeed unless they have courage that grows out of a relationship with God in prayer and reflection.

7. *Nehemiah planned with foresight.* Effective leaders think ahead and plan their course of action carefully. This Nehemiah did.

8. *Nehemiah understood God's gracious favour on him.* Leaders are responsible to plan, but they fully recognise that plans only succeed with God's gracious favour.

9. *Nehemiah did extensive research.* Read the book of Nehemiah and discover a leader who did extensive research before giving direction. He toured the walls at night to examine the problem before giving orders.

10. *Nehemiah displayed a decisive will and call to action.* Leaders must not only think and pray, plan and research, they must be decisive and act like a leader. Courageous decisions must be made, and Nehemiah did just that.

11. *Nehemiah was a leader with followers.* No one is going to follow leaders who do not know or are unsure of themselves. A decisive and confident leader draws followers. A leader by definition is someone who has followers and Nehemiah had followers who built the wall of Jerusalem.

12. *Nehemiah was a capable organiser of people.* Planning involves a *dream* of the future, but unless the leader can organise people to do something, the futuristic dream will remain only a dream. Nehemiah knew how to organise the people in building the wall.

13. *Nehemiah overcame hindrances*. Opposition from without and from within is inevitable. Nehemiah experienced many hindrances, but he overcame them through perseverance, patience, and courage.

An effective Christian leader is exemplified by Nehemiah who had both deep faith and trust in God as well as a recognition of his own responsibility. Notice Nehemiah's response when faced by his enemies: "And they all plotted together to come and fight against Jerusalem . . . And we prayed to our God and set a guard as protection against them day and night" (Nehemiah 4:8-9).

7

Management Skills of Christian Leaders

Leadership skills include the ability to manage. Unless a Christian leader knows how to manage, he or she cannot succeed. Management is all about vision, setting goals, organising resources, setting schedules, directing, and controlling so that the goals are accomplished. Without management skills a leader will lead aimlessly. This chapter deals with four ingredients in management.

DEVELOPING RELATIONSHIPS

Developing relationships is foundational for all management. African proverbs teach the importance of teamwork with the whole community pulling together. One African proverb says: "You cannot play a drum with one finger." The Yoruba and Igbo of Nigeria say: "It takes a whole village to raise a child." The Kuria of Kenya say: "One person is thin porridge; two or three people are a handful of ugali" (stiff cooked meal).

How do we develop relationships? Following is a summary of the recommendations made by African Christian leaders who have learned these lessons in ministry.

1. *Respect everyone, even your opponents.* It is good to esteem others better than yourself. To honour someone is to recognise the other person's worth. Value and respect team members because of their performance and achievement. In public and private give them expressions of praise, esteem, appreciation, affirmation, approval, and commendation.
2. *Show love and kindness to your team members.* Love is basic when developing personal relationships. This includes care and compassion for those in need.

Friendship is an expression of love. Show them honour through non-verbal means such as the tone of voice, the look of the eyes, and the expression of the face, all reflecting genuineness and sincerity.

3. *Learn to know your team members.* Down deep inside every person has a desire to be known. When someone does understand us, we feel accepted and loved. Yet the compelling desire to be known is not matched by the desire to know others because of our incurable selfishness. As Saint Francis of Assisi prayed: "Let me not seek to be understood but to understand." This requires visiting them in their homes and informally.
4. *Accept people as they are.* A leader must recognise the quirks, wrinkles, and idiosyncrasies of each person. We are all different in our personalities with strengths and weaknesses which attract or repel. A leader must learn to accept people as they are and not focus on their weaknesses.
5. *Show a personal interest in team members.* People are not merely workers who contribute toward the goals of the institution. They are *people* and people need a personal touch. Greet them. Sincerely inquire of their well-being. When a leader seeks to meet the felt needs, they will reciprocate by respecting the leader and cooperating.
6. *Cultivate a trusting relationship.* If leaders are to succeed, they must be able to trust their team members and team members must be able to trust their leader. Character and competence of the leader are necessary for team members to trust their leader. Integrity, honesty, truthfulness, purity, and humility are essential, as well as competence in leadership.
7. *Share your vision with your team members.* A leader must rally the team members around the vision embraced by the team. Because some may develop reservations or doubts concerning the vision, the leader should continually refresh the fire that kindled the acceptance of the vision.
8. *Work together as a team.* Nothing brings a leader closer to the people than standing shoulder to shoulder and working together with the people. A wise leader demonstrates how to do something by being part of the team in doing it. This relationship with the team makes it easier to gently correct those who are lagging behind.
9. *Never embarrass people.* It is one thing for the leader to correct in private. It is another to make people lose face by correcting them in the front of others. *How* a leader corrects is critical. *Never* correct in public.

10. *Use a personal touch in directing people*. Issuing instructions through the impersonal means of paper or electronics is not being personal. A faceless instruction is less compelling than a face-to-face encounter.
11. *Be gracious in leadership*. People almost always fall short of the leader's expectations. For the sake of maintaining harmonious relationships, it is important to move forward together as a team and this requires a leader who is gracious and considerate in all of his or her dealings with the team.
12. *Assist the team members to develop their gifts*. Everyone likes to grow and develop to reach their God-given potential. When a leader shows a personal interest by helping team members to improve their skills by sending them to seminars or offering a training course, they will appreciate their leader.
13. *Be fair to everyone*. Favouritism does not breed unity, nor does it motivate. Every worker should experience a sense of justice and equality.

PLANNING

Leaders plan to fail whenever they fail to plan. The tragedy is that planning never takes place for many leaders. Their approach to leadership is to deal with crises whenever they arise. Failed leaders are forever dealing with problems instead of planning how to develop a flourishing ministry.

Importance of Planning

Learning to plan is not alien to African tradition. Some people believe that long-term planning was not done by Africans traditionally. Certainly, long-term planning as outlined in this book was unknown, but Africans did plan for the distant future. Blessings on their families were pronounced by old men with the distant future in mind. Plans for marriage of their children were made by fathers before the children were born. Men planned for large families and rich estates in their quest for an influential clan in the future.

Some Christians today reject planning with goal setting because they think planning replaces the guidance of the Holy Spirit. But should not the Holy Spirit guide one in planning? Jesus himself commended the planning of builders and warriors (Luke 14:28-33). He denounced foolish people who fail to think ahead (Matthew 7:24-27). Paul challenges Christians to emulate the athlete who plans and organises for winning an athletic contest (1 Corinthians 9:24-27). Planning is both biblical and necessary for leaders.

Planning involves two essential elements:

- Develop a *vision* of God's will for the future.
- Develop specific *goals* with detailed steps to fulfil the vision.

Planning Always Begins with a Vision

A vision is a picture of your future dreams of what you pray will be accomplished in the future. A vision is a general statement that cannot be measured. A Christian vision or a sanctified dream of the future is:

- *God-imparted*: The leader and team pray and seek God's will.
- *Change-oriented*: Dissatisfied with the present, it seeks change.
- *Action-oriented*: Without action taken, the vision is not achieved.
- *Both faith-based and realistic*: The vision is large enough to require faith but not so large that it is realistically impossible.

All Christian planning for the future must begin with an inspired vision of future changes desired after much prayer and discussion by the team led by the Christian leader. This vision should create unity of purpose in future activities while inspiring and motivating the team in united action. Ideally the vision statement creates enthusiasm in accomplishing the vision.

Several steps are taken to develop a vision. Leaders must lead their teams in thoughtful, reflective prayer for God's will. Gather information of what God is doing elsewhere. The teams discuss because many minds are better than one. However, leaders should take the lead by thinking and suggesting, but not controlling the decisions. Answer the question *why* your church/Christian organisation exists? *Why* you want change? Then write down the statement on paper in one phrase or simple sentence.

Examples of a vision statement include "Our church will be known as an evangelistically minded church" or "The single adults in our church will feel nurtured and loved."

Planning Requires *Goal Setting*

Once a vision is stated, goals are required to show how you will achieve the vision. Goal setting moves from ethereal dreams to concrete specifics.

- *Goals are stated in terms of end results.* For example: By the end of this year, I will finish reading the Bible from beginning to the end.

- *Goals are achievable in a definite time period.* All goals have an ending date for accomplishment.
- *Goals are definite as to what is expected.* For example: "By the end of this course, students will have read the following three books (give titles and authors of books)." A goal that says "The goal of this course is for students to read several books on management" breaks all the above stated principles.
- *Goals are practical and realistic.* Not too easy and not too hard.
- *Goals should be written with simplicity.* Limit one goal per statement. Use a simple sentence, not complex or compound.

Having an end goal is not sufficient. Intermediate steps are needed to achieve the end goal. These goals must then be arranged in sequential steps.

- *Arrange a programme of activities and personnel needed to achieve the goals.* What personnel are needed and what activities need to take place?
- *Arrange a schedule of when the different activities will be accomplished.* Be practical! Nothing will be accomplished without planning on the time when certain things are accomplished. Adjustments can always be made later if necessary.
- *Arrange a budget to cater for the needs of the programme of action.* A budget includes personnel, finance, and other resources. Therefore, a careful accounting must be made to achieve the vision and stated goals.

ORGANISING

Organising people in a structure must follow the first step of planning. Vision is an empty dream unless the leader can mobilize people in a workable structure so that everyone pulls together to accomplish the goals. As a Swahili proverb says, "If birds travel without coordination, they beat each other's wings."

Without organising, some tasks might be overlooked, and other tasks would have an excessive number of workers. Conflicts can arise when members do not know their precise assignment and how it relates to others.[9]

What Is Organising?

Organising is the process of assigning team members a particular ministry to contribute toward achieving certain goals by arranging them in an *orderly structure*.

An organisational structure holds the team members together in an orderly manner, just as a steel skeleton holds a tall building together. The organisational structure shows how each teammate relates to the other teammates in a prearranged organisation. It indicates who is responsible to whom. Sometimes called a flow chart, the organisational structure is a command structure which indicates who has authority over whom and to whom a person is responsible.

How Do You Organise?

Whenever a person is chosen to be a leader in the church, a theological institution, or a ministry organisation, it is most likely that an organisational structure is already in place. The wise leader will first serve within that structure and develop relationships with the teammates. Only after some time and experience should he or she think of improving, adapting, or changing the organisational structure. It may be that a project arises which needs volunteers to join together to accomplish a task. Following are some principles to follow in developing an organisational structure or flow chart.

1. *Clarify the vision and goals of the organisation* before the organisational structure is developed. Strategy comes before structure. Only when you know precisely what God wants you to do can you then develop a structure that will serve everyone.
2. *Organise with natural groupings in mind.* Think of the different categories of your team members – ages, genders, education, occupation, gifts, or home locations.
3. *Be specific when assigning ministries.* Job descriptions should specify identifiable work assignments which can be examined and evaluated. To say that a groundsman is responsible to care for the compound is too vague. Specify what he should do and how often it should be done.
4. *Draw an organisational chart on paper,* using rectangular blocks to represent groups or persons functioning in certain capacities. Be clear on the qualifications for each position outlined. Draw vertical lines showing who is subordinate to another and who is responsible to whom. If the organisational chart is flat, then too many people report to the leader, and this will wear out the leader. If the organisational chart is too deep with too many subordinates overseeing people, then the leader is too far removed from the team members on the ground, and he becomes isolated from the actual work on the ground. Below is an example of an organisational chart. From this sample you can creatively devise an organisational chart for your own ministry.

Nonprofit Organizational Chart

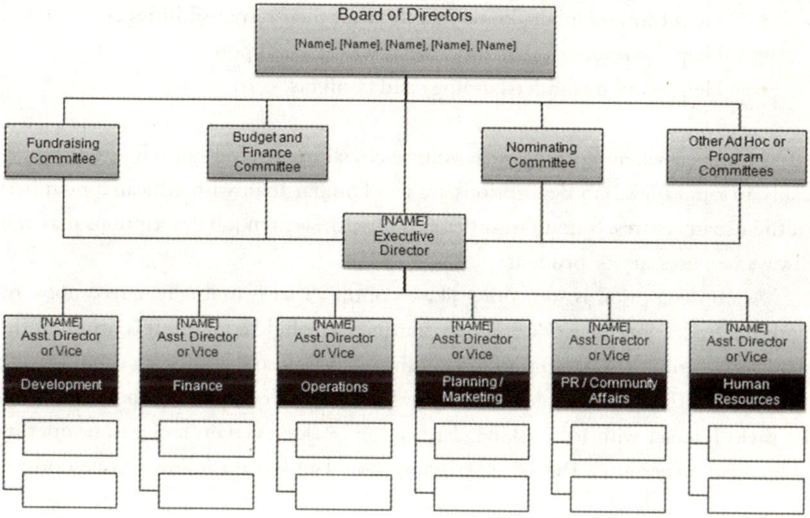

5. *Write on paper all the names of the available personnel.* Briefly describe their strengths, weaknesses, and previous experience. People have unique personalities, interests, and abilities. A wise leader recognises that individual team members can do some things well and others things not so well. To build up the team members and the organisation, every person must be placed where she or he can serve best.
6. *Place the names of the qualified persons in the organisational chart*, beginning from the top. Always match the person's strengths and proven experience with the needed qualifications for each position on the organisational chart, and always consult with the person for his or her consent.
7. *Write a job description for each person on the chart* (see below).
8. *Remember, all organising is a process.* This means that no organisational structure is permanent or unchangeable. As the organisation grows or changes, it will be necessary to grow and change the structure.

Job Descriptions

Writing job descriptions is an important part of organising. Job descriptions are absolutely essential for employees within institutions, ministry organisations, and urban churches.

Job descriptions are important because they:

- Help team members know exactly what their responsibilities are.
- Help the leader to remember what was agreed upon.
- Help avoid misunderstandings and conflicts.

However, when working with volunteers within a local church setting, especially in rural ones, job descriptions are less familiar than with educated members in the urban centres. Situations differ and formal, written job descriptions may not always be necessary or prudent.

A job description is something like a contract that is mutually agreed upon by both the leader and the worker. When drafting the job description, it is helpful if the workers contribute to the composition of the document so that they are committed to what it says. The leader should present a draft of the job description to the workers and let them interact with it by asking clarification, making certain requests, or offering alternative suggestions. The job description should answer the following questions:

1. What are my responsibilities? (What is my job?)
2. What authority do I have? (What am I authorized to do?)
3. To whom do I look for directions? (Who is my boss?)
4. Who looks to me for direction? (Who reports to me?)

Every job description has the following elements:

1. Title – title of the position
2. Purpose – the purpose of the position
3. Scope – the extent of responsibility
4. Areas of responsibility and authority
5. Working relationships – the person you report to, the persons who report to you and those you work closely together with should all be indicated

Delegation

Delegation is the assigning of certain tasks and authority to carry out those tasks to some other team member. These tasks are in addition to the ones found in the job description. The leader takes one of her or his own responsibilities and delegates it to another person to carry out that task.

Delegation is essential if leaders desire to be successful. If leaders take on too much work, they will burn out. Delegating work responsibilities to others distributes the work so that no one is overworked.

Many leaders, however, fear to delegate because they fear giving up their authority. They may even fear others will do the work better than themselves and therefore their leadership is threatened. Many leaders are perfectionists, and they fear others will not do the job as well as they want.

How does a leader delegate?

1. Decide what should be delegated.
2. Choose the right person for the task.
3. Transfer the *work* to a person willing to take on the task.
4. Transfer the *authority* for doing the work.
5. Follow up with encouragement and assistance when needed.

Leaders often fail when delegating work because:

1. They fail to give full authority to do the work. Frustration arises.
2. They fail to define what authority they don't have. Conflict arises.
3. They fail to define clearly what is delegated. Confusion develops.
4. They fail to invest the time and effort required to observe, teach, listen, and follow-up, all of which are necessary for successful delegation. Failure occurs. This takes time and effort.
5. They take back the work assigned because they are perfectionists and feel the work was not done satisfactorily.

Management skills include planning with vision and goals, and the making of an organisational structured. But more is needed – shepherding and guiding team members toward accomplishing the goals.

SHEPHERDING

Leading a team to accomplish objectives doesn't just happen. It takes work. As the Kamba say: "Fatty meat doesn't chew itself." Achieving goals doesn't happen without serious effort on the part of the leader.

Once leaders and their team members agree on a vision statement with goals and an organisational structure to accomplish those goals is prepared, the leaders need to shepherd their team members to accomplish the goals.

Traditionally, this phase of management is referred to as *directing* and *controlling*, a process of ensuring that the performance of the workers is according to plan. The leader supervises and controls the work so that the goals are achieved. But *directing* and *controlling*, are authoritarian terms that frequently entail confrontation – not an appropriate concept for the African context.

For this reason, instead of *controlling* we have chosen the term, *shepherding* because it is more biblical and more pastoral – less authoritarian and confrontational, though both ideas are embedded in shepherding. The oriental shepherd did not drive the sheep as Africans do, but led the sheep. Even so leaders achieve their goals not by driving team members, but by leading them and modelling for their followers what should be done.

In Africa the cultures are more people oriented, less goal oriented. So, do we have a conflict between Western ideas and African values? The Christian leaders we consulted all admitted that *directing* and *controlling* (or what we would call *shepherding*) are indeed a challenge, but believed it is still possible and desirable. In fact, planning and time orientation were found in the people-oriented cultures of traditional Africa as we have seen. In some cultures, the father in the home kept an office where he counselled and settled disputes. He always had time for everyone but did not allow a few people to take all of his time. Goals were set and met.

Shepherding in Africa is possible when the following conditions are met:

1. *The team members are involved in every stage of the planning.*
2. *The team members own the project.* If they see the project as yours as the leader, they may not embrace it. But if it is their project, they will accept shepherding.
3. *The team members are guided, not commanded.* Relationships are important. Leaders can and must shepherd their people, but this requires people-skills in knowing how to guide and correct.

Shepherding by *Motivation*

Motivating the team members must be a priority for the leader. If leaders are to *lead* their team members, not to drive them, they must be motivated.

A motivation prompts a person to do something. It gives the person a reason for doing it. This may be the proverbial carrot to entice faithful work or stick to warn of punishment – a threat of consequences if work is not done, or a reward if work is well done. The best motive, however, is a positive motivation to encourage morale of the workers.

Affirm Team Members

Team members need to feel respected and affirmed and this can be done in four ways:

1. *Acceptance.* If one is accepted, he or she is included within the team as one of "us". The person feels respected. Favouritism or exclusion shows rejection.
2. *Trust.* A person's morale is boosted when the leader shows trust in the person. When the leader neglects or overlooks someone by not entrusting him or her with responsibility, this demoralizes the person.
3. *Reward.* This can be shown by a personal word of praise, a public commendation, certificate of recognition, or a material gift.
4. *Support.* A leader who cares for the needs of team members by offering appropriate support when needed, builds up a team member.

Communicate Verbally

By far the best way to motivate people is to communicate with words of praise and thanks. Compliment them when they do well and congratulate them when they complete a project. Pray with them. If they become discouraged, speak words of encouragement. Remind them of the mutually agreed upon goals and encourage them to strive towards them. Personal communication is far better than notes or email.

Provide Tangible Gestures of Appreciation

Verbal expressions of appreciation may be accompanied by gifts, certificates, or food and fellowship.

Share Yourself and Offer Yourself as a Model

When leaders are transparent and share their own life, their relationship with God, their struggles and secret of success, team members are motivated by the leaders' example. This can best be done when visiting your workers in their own homes. Several Christian leaders shared their experience:

- I give younger pastors my history and tell them all about my past; I share concerning the little salary I received as a younger pastor. This greatly encourages them. To show the road you travelled encourages them.
- For many years I served in the largest church in our church region. When I was elected as the chairman of the church region, I requested to be assigned a smaller church. Now I leave at 4:30 a.m. to walk two hours to the church for the 7:00 a.m. prayer meeting.

The lives of these servant-leaders model a humble servant of God which motivates the pastors under them to do the same.

Motivation Killers

If leaders take a real interest in their team members and express that concern with the various suggestions given above, they will surely motivate the members – *unless* the leaders actually kill motivation by some foolish acts. Leaders should *never* do the following:

- Belittle a subordinate
- Criticise a subordinate in front of others
- Fail to give subordinates your undivided attention
- Seem to be preoccupied with your own interests
- Play favourites
- Be insensitive to small things
- Embarrass weaker employees

Shepherding by *Communicating*

One of the primary reasons for leadership failure is a breakdown in communication. When the leader fails to communicate, motivation suffers.

Unity within the community is impossible without effective communication. You feel left out when things happen around you without being told. You feel demoralized and become critical and negative. Confusion arises when people don't know what is expected of them. When the leader fails to communicate clearly the goals set before them, members lose their focus and commitment.

Leaders fail to communicate adequately for a variety of reasons:

- Leaders do not understand the importance of communication.
- Leaders are lazy and make no effort to communicate.
- Leaders protect their power through secrecy. Knowledge is power.
- Leaders *assume* that everyone knows.
- Leaders do not take the time to listen. Listening is an important part of communication because uttering pronouncements (giving out information) is not communication. A leader cannot *assume* the people understand. The process of communication involves both the speaker and receiver. Those who hear the pronouncement may understand it differently than what is intended. A leader must obtain feedback from the people to ensure that people heard correctly. Ask the person to state what his or her understanding is.

The best principles of communicating include:

1. *Develop a strong personal relationship with all your team.* The better they know you, the better they will understand you – and vice versa. Demonstrate love for them. Be friendly, polite, and kind.
2. *Face-to-face communication is the best.* Though written communication may be the simplest, talking face-to-face pays rich dividends. Only 7 per cent of understanding comes from understanding the words. Tone of voice and body language are much more important. It is far better to speak to people personally than to send a notice.
3. *Communicate with people informally.* The good leader mingles with the workers and informally chats with them. When talking with them in their homes outside the formalities of an office, this helps.
4. *Prepare carefully when speaking to large audiences.* Know the audience. Smaller groups are better because you can get feedback.
5. *Desire feedback.* Listen carefully to the feedback. Ask questions. Ask them to repeat in their own words what you have told them. This will help the leader know whether he or she was understood correctly.
6. *Always be sincere.* Sincerity with humility builds trust.
7. *Be generous when communicating with team members.* Don't be stingy with information given. Don't allow members to learn by surprises. Don't expect them to hear from others what you said.
8. *Always be transparent and close to the people.* Staying at a distance can only create suspicion and misunderstanding. Rumours and gossip abound in the absence of personal, face-to-face communication.

Shepherding by *Correcting*

For the Christian leader to shepherd the team so that they will work together and accomplish goals, it requires not only motivational and communication skills but an ability to correct those who need correction. Painful times will come when the leader must correct the errant sheep.

The work of a shepherd in feeding and guiding the sheep is enjoyable. Many African leaders have told me so. But even shepherds carrry a club which they find necessary to use when correcting the errant sheep.

Correcting a team member is difficult in any culture, but especially in cultures that are shame-oriented and people-centred. One leader even told me that correcting is an African problem because of the cultural pressures that cause most leaders to avoid confrontation. *Correcting* is so difficult that many leaders ignore the problem, even when it involves a sin.

But after talking with leaders in Kenya, we have concluded that with wisdom, correcting *can be done*, and it *must* be done. Following are some thoughts on how shepherd-leaders may correct those who are not fulfilling their responsibilities. The accent of this book, however, is on the positive. When the leader emphasizes the positive, the correcting will be easier.

Suggestions for Making Corrections

When correcting is necessary the following suggestions will help. Many of these are repetitive, but they form the foundation on which correction is possible.

1. *Develop strong, personal relationships with every team member*. When all members respect and trust their leader – and even like their leader – they will be open to correction that is given in a positive and affirming manner.
2. *Include all the team members in the process of setting goals*. If the members participate in the process of setting goals, they will be more committed to doing their part in fulfilling the goals.
3. *Include all the team members in drawing up a programme to achieve those goals.* It may be easier and quicker for the leader to do all the planning, but the implementation will be more difficult if the members did not have a say in developing the programme.
4. *Train the team members so that they know how to do their work.* Leaders must be servants and come down to the level of their team members, in order to show them what to do. Be a servant! Demonstrate practically how to do it. As a result of the training, the workers will do their work better and love their leader who helped them.
5. *Help the team members enjoy their work.* They need to know that their leader is happy with them and that God is pleased with their work. Remind them that above all they are serving God who will reward them.
6. *Use the Word of God when instructing them.* The Christian leader is wise to use the Scriptures. The Bible is rich with instruction on the importance of diligent work, as in the Proverbs.
7. *Stay close to those to whom work is delegated.* A major mistake which leaders make is to abandon their team members once a work assignment has been entrusted to them. Stay close to them, ask how they are doing and help them whenever necessary.

8. *Leaders must be consumed with the vision to complete the task.* The leader is the key and must stay on top of things. The leader must keep people moving forward by instilling the vision of accomplishing the goals, by inspiring them to work with words of encouragement, and by helping them overcome some difficulty they are having.
9. *The actual task of correcting requires interpersonal skills.* This is the more difficult part of being a leader. Many leaders have a difficult time of correcting effectively. Correcting is possible but only with social skills. Correct in such a way that the team member is both corrected and remains a friend.
10. *Begin correcting by speaking to the whole team in general terms.* Though the leader may know who in particular needs correction, by speaking to the whole group in general he or she avoids embarrassing the individual. Make a general correction.
11. *Begin talking to individuals personally by asking questions.* Never begin from a judgmental attitude. Don't assume you know that the person is wrong. Find out what made the person do what she or he did. If the person has a reasonable excuse, the leader should forgive.
12. *Be wise and respectful when correcting.* The language of correction must be laced with kindness, respect, and wisdom. Don't speak of "you" but "we" and "us" because the leader and worker are in this together. See value in the person and seek to help him or her. Give due respect to an older person. Always remember the wisdom of the African sages. A Kamba proverb says: "Water once spilt cannot be collected again." Words spoken rashly and in anger can never be taken back, even with apologies.
13. *Never embarrass a team member before others.* Never criticise or correct them in front of others. One leader said to me, "I don't mind my work being criticised, but I don't want to lose face or be embarrassed."
14. *Always correct the person privately and in love.* If you love a person and the relationship is good, he or she will know that your correction is for his or her good.
15. *Never erupt in anger or rage.* Leaders must master their feelings.
16. *Always speak the truth in love and be sensitive and loving, though firm.* Never compromise the truth; but speaking the truth must be done in a loving manner.

Following these guidelines, the shepherd can lead the team toward completing the goals and achieve the vision laid out with prayerful thought.

8

Issues for Christian Leaders

Life with its responsibilities of leadership is a lifelong marathon, not a short sprint. Certain issues must be mastered by the Christian leader in order to remain effective over the long haul. Following are key issues.

A BALANCED LIFESTYLE

An imbalanced lifestyle will lead eventually to a failure in leadership. Nothing is more important to understand than this: a leader is not "the Almighty." A leader cannot do everything. Only a fool pretends to be what he or she is not. Limited time in a day, limited strength and energy, limited gifts, and limited opportunities coupled with many demands press upon every leader.

Philosophy of a Balanced Lifestyle

Balancing a lifestyle must grow out of the following basic premises.

1. *Balancing your lifestyle is a life-long challenge.*

   First, a balanced lifestyle is not a choice between good and evil. Life is full of many good things to do. But given our limitations, we must prioritize what is the most important for which God has gifted us and called us to do.

   Second, balancing a lifestyle is a challenge because situations change continually – your child suddenly becomes sick, a major misunderstanding arises in the ministry, a building project consumes more time than planned.

2. *Balancing your lifestyle, though a challenge, is essential.* If you desire to be effective, you have no alternative. *Your body* will deteriorate if you neglect it. *Your relationship with God* will suffer if you don't maintain a consistent walk with the Lord in prayer and Bible study. *Your family* will suffer if you neglect them. *Your ministry* will not prosper as it should if you neglect your responsibilities.

3. *Balancing your lifestyle requires biblical priorities.* If we are to love our neighbours as ourselves, this means we must care for ourselves in a loving and careful manner – spiritually, physically, mentally, and relationally.

Essentials of a Balanced Lifestyle

Given the limitations of time, physical strength, and material resources, every Christian leader must consider how best to fulfil those responsibilities. It is not a question of choosing between all that is important. *Doing good is imperative. Doing everything is impossible.*

Following are the essentials for a biblically balanced lifestyle if you are to love God with all your heart, love your neighbour as yourself, and care for yourself and your family.

Cultivate a Personal Relationship with the Lord

One young leader told me: "I have not really balanced my lifestyle. Balancing is very hard. The ministry is overwhelming the spiritual side. This is very hard. I need more self-discipline. Ministry takes most of my time." Indeed, his ministry is prospering, but unless this dear brother deals with this imbalance, he is headed for barrenness, professionalism, and spiritual failure.

Attend to the Needs of Your Body and Mind

Medical knowledge and medicines are reducing the sicknesses that were endemic throughout Africa in the past. But tragically, the Western lifestyle and diet has penetrated Africa so that people are becoming sick with Western diseases of diabetes, heart disease, cancer, and hypertension (high blood pressure). Instead of walking long distances, people live a sedentary life. Instead of eating traditional cereals, they eat white bread and drink soda and tea saturated with sugar. Obesity, being overweight, is the result.

The solution is daily aerobic exercise and a balanced diet with protein (nuts, beans, meat, eggs, and cheese), fibre (whole grains, vegetables, beans, and certain fruits), carbohydrates that come from nuts, vegetables, and whole grains rather than candy, white bread, cakes, and drinks filled with sugar.

Developing the mind is also essential. Woe to the leaders who think that Bible school or college is all they need. Keep growing in learning by reading and studying to remain fresh and up to date.

Love and Care for Your Spouse, Children, and Extended Family

A chaplain in Kenya told me: "It is important to take care of your family. Develop your family. When you are in trouble, your family provides the cushion. Love your wife, be good to her, and develop real fellowship with her and your children. When others reject you, your family is your refuge."

Faithfully Serve God in Your Place of Ministry

Most Christian leaders focus on ministry, but always remember you are serving God first and foremost, not people who can be demanding and unappreciative. Devote yourself to training and equipping others so you can delegate some of the ministry to them. Don't do the work of ten men. Rather, train ten men to do the work with you.

Relate to Your Community, Society, and Government as Salt and Light

Leaders must determine what their role is in the larger community. Whatever your position in ministry, seek to find your place of contribution in the wider community as a living witness to Jesus Christ.

SELF-DISCIPLINE

"Every athlete exercises self-control in all things . . . I discipline my body and keep it under control" (1 Corinthians 9:25, 279:25, 27). Every successful leader is self-disciplined.

What Is Self-Discipline?

Self-discipline is self-policing, self-management, and self-control. While children need adults to oversee them to ensure proper conduct, self-disciplined leaders govern themselves to do what should be done.

A successful athlete learns to exercise self-control, to discipline his or her body, and focus on winning the game. Likewise, a self-disciplined leader has learned to be laser-focused on Jesus Christ to please him and do his will.

What Should Be the *Motive* for Self-Discipline?

Athletes competed in the ancient Greek Olympics in order to win a prize, a crown of leaves from an olive tree – highly treasured but perishable. Many Christian leaders exercise self-discipline, motivated by their desire to advance themselves and achieve fame and fortune. Such self-centred motives are unworthy of a child of God.

True servants of the Lord are motivated in ministry by their love for the Lord Jesus who saved them from eternal damnation and called them into divine service. After Peter's fateful denial of Jesus, he encountered the Lord on the beach after going to fish all night without catching a thing. Jesus asked Peter: "Do you love me more than these?" When Peter affirmed his love, Jesus told him: "Feed my sheep." This exchange occurred three times: "Do you love me? Feed my sheep! (read John 21:1-19). Our love for Jesus is expressed in our obedience in doing his will.

Paul disciplined himself "for the sake of the gospel" (1 Corinthians 9:23). In fact, Paul exclaimed: "Woe to me if I do not preach the gospel!" (1 Corinthians 9:16). Because of our love for Jesus who rescued us from the dominion of darkness, we are obligated to obey the Lord in all things.

The Lord has promised to reward his servants with an imperishable crown (1 Corinthians 9:25, NIV) based on their faithfulness, not on their public acclaim or human success (Matthew 25:21).

Paul states that "it is *required* that those who have been given a trust must prove *faithful*" (1 Corinthians 4:2, NIV, emphasis mine). How does one serve *faithfully*?

Faithful leaders go beyond the call of duty. They see what needs to be done and take on additional work. Faithful leaders are trustworthy, always looking after the welfare of the church and the glory of the Saviour, and not the selfish gains of a self-centred leader. Faithless leaders limit their work to the minimal expectations of others. They refuse to serve beyond the minimal obligations unless they receive extra payment of money. Faithful leaders pour themselves into their calling without consideration of pay or reward, for their eyes are on pleasing the Lord and eternal rewards.

How Do Self-Disciplined Leaders Manage Their Time?

Many live under the tyranny of the urgent. Needs arise that demand immediate attention. Leaders become stressed out because of the pressure of obligations.

What every Christian leader must consider is that time is a gift from our heavenly Father – an opportunity to serve him. God has granted life and strength, and opportunities for each day. The gift of time is equally distributed to everyone – just 24 hours in every day, no more and no less. The question is: "How will you use the time allotted to you?"

Steve Chalke (*Managing Your Time*) offers these helpful suggestions:

- *Begin by setting your goals and priorities.* What *must* be done today and what can wait for another day if need be?
- *Prioritize your activities!* Make sure that the most important things are done first. Ask yourself, "What would happen if this were not done today or at all?"
- *Be flexible.* Learn to delegate. The overstressed leader must always ask, "Which of the matters that calls for my attention could be done by someone else?" The solution to overwork is delegation and better planning.

- *Avoid distractions.* Time-wasters include prolonged socializing, lost focus on the goals, failure to communicate properly, procrastination, lack of discipline, excessive use of the cell phone, and too much talking. Learn to redeem the time.
- *Fight stress!* Chalk advises that you slow down, be realistic, learn to say no, take time to reflect, enjoy yourself, take care of yourself, and get a balance with quieter times to allow the body to revitalize.

Tied together in one bundle are self-discipline, time management, and a balanced lifestyle. No one can lead a balanced lifestyle unless you exercise self-discipline in your time management. First, cultivate your relationship with God. Second, attend to the need of your body and mind. Family should never be short-changed for ministry. Never neglect your spouse and children. Ministry can be all-consuming, but the leader must cut the job down to size so that none of the above-stated priorities are neglected.

MAINTAINING UNITY

The Scripture teaches: "Make every effort to keep the unity of the Spirit through the bond of peace" (Ephesians 4:3, NIV). A major challenge for the Christian leader is to maintain unity among diverse individuals.

Disunity, if left unresolved, will simmer into a major crisis. The Christian community does not need more leaders with academic degrees or charismatic personalities. What it needs is Christian leaders filled with love and humility and gifted with relational skills to bring factions together.

There are many kinds of conflict. Most conflicts are over *personal issues*. Other conflicts are *material in nature*, struggles over property rights and garden disputes. Unhappiness arises over salary, fringe benefits, and housing. Conflicts often occur over *change* which people do not like. On other occasions conflict arises over *ideological or theological differences*. These latter differences can be the most difficult to handle.

Importance of Unity

Before Jesus's death on the cross he prayed specifically for the eleven apostles and for all those who would believe thereafter, praying:

> I pray . . . that all of them may be one, Father, just as you are in me and I am in you . . . that they may be one as we are one . . . that they may be brought to complete unity. Then the world will

> know that you sent me and have loved them even as you have loved me (John 17:21-23, NIV).

Jesus did not pray that they might have great power to preach and heal. He did not pray that they would be successful in their evangelism and in the planting of many churches. He prayed for *unity*. Jesus knew what was in the human heart. He saw his own disciples clash with each other.

Unity is of great importance because love and unity draw people to Christ. The world is full of conflict. If the church is no different from the world, why should others believe in Christ? Furthermore, Christian leaders need a united people if they are to lead them to do great exploits for Christ. A divided house cannot stand.

But unity is not uniformity, the absence of different opinions. Differences of opinions can be healthy when handled with respectful, loving, and open minds. But when people do not listen to one another with respect and do not submit to the wisdom of the group, then destructive conflict arises.

Principles of Conflict Resolution

Following are some biblical and contextually appropriate principles which Christian leaders can use to help resolve conflict whenever it arises.

1. *Seek resolution quickly*. Frequently, leaders let misunderstandings continue without resolution, but this is not healthy. Many small problems become complex and more difficult to resolve when not solved quickly.
2. *Use loving, humble, and gentle words*. The Bible is clear: "A soft answer turns away wrath, but a harsh word stirs up anger" (Proverbs 15:1). No one can bring reconciliation with harsh, unkind, judgmental words.
3. *Begin reconciliation efforts with the two offended*. Conflict can best be resolved when done immediately by the two in conflict. Understanding helps bring reconciliation. If the person who caused offence would humble himself or herself and apologize, the matter can be resolved quickly.
4. *If reconciliation fails, make another attempt, this time with other companions*. This is the biblical approach (Matthew 18:16). Both should seek to understand the other, using kind and gentle words, rather than being defensive or judgmental.
5. *Take steps for personal, private reconciliation*. Depending on the nature of the conflict, the offended party may need to take the mature, Christian approach by "forgiving" that person unilaterally. If the other person cannot admit

wrongdoing, the offended person should not allow himself or herself to become bitter and resentful.

These first five principles assume that the two individuals are mature in their Christian faith and well taught. These principles should be taught by the Christian leader so that they will be practiced by everyone.

6. *The Christian leader has a particular responsibility in conflict resolution.* Many times the leader must step in with extraordinary measures. How else will disagreements be resolved apart from the leader?
7. *A mediator should be found who is acceptable to both factions.* The best mediators are usually found within the group, for they know all the cultural nuances of the problem. This takes great wisdom for they must be skilled in making communication easier.
8. *The aim of mediation should be reconciliation and restoration.* Use of mediation is the traditional African method and the aim is consensus to avoid winners and losers. But if sin has occurred, then confession and repentance is required. If very serious, like adultery, then discipline is required.
9. *The mediator should normally act through the council of elders.* Though the mediator should be an authority figure, he or she should normally work through a council of elders.
10. *The mediator should be well informed.* The better the mediator understands the problem, the better he or she is able to help reconcile.

GROWING A LEADER IN CHARACTER

"We are to grow up in every way into him who is the head, into Christ" (Ephesians 4:15). No worthy leader stops learning! We must all keep growing. Here Robert Clinton (*The Making of a Leader*) is helpful.

Over 37 years we have followed with keen interest those whom we had the privilege of mentoring and helping to prepare for Christian ministry. After some time, a few have dropped by the wayside, stumbling on issues of character. Others have continued on in ministry, faithfully serving, but plateaued in their skills of ministry. An encouraging number have continued to learn and grow. They have been focused and disciplined, maturing in ministry. Continual learning and growing is the key.

It is both encouraging and challenging to remember that *no* leader becomes what he or she is destined to be without continual learning in life and ministry. *No* effective leader ceases to learn until God takes the leader home.

In many ways these last two sections will be a summary of the book because the lessons we learn throughout life are repeated to bring maturity. The basic foundation on which all Christian leadership is built is *character*. All the African Christian leaders whom we interviewed have said this.

Self-Examination

Are you growing? Are you all that God has designed you to be? Following are some basic principles with questions that you should ask yourself to determine whether you are really growing as God's servant.

1. *The Word of God Principle:* Do I have a growing appetite to read, study, memorize, and obey the Word of God?
2. *The Prayer Principle:* Do I spend meaningful time each day in communion with God in prayer – worshipping, confessing, and interceding for others? Do I find joy and satisfaction in my relationship with God?
3. *The Humility Principle:* Do others see me as a humble servant-leader whose primary desire is to serve God and others, or am I self-centred?
4. *The Love Principle:* Am I jealous of others who have larger churches, bigger salaries, "higher" positions or greater "success" in ministry? Do I increasingly show characteristics of love with kindness and patience?
5. *The Holiness Principle:* Is my life marked by a thirst for righteousness and holiness and a desire to live in obedience to God's Word? Is my living consistent with my preaching? Do I practice what I preach?
6. *The Self-Discipline Principle:* Am I increasingly self-disciplined, living a balanced lifestyle?
7. *The Faithfulness Principle:* Do I serve with joy, offering all my service as unto God?

We all fall short in one way or another, but the crucial issue is whether we desire to keep on growing. Growth in character takes place when we immerse ourselves in God's Word and delight ourselves in prayer.

Growing Character through Adversity

Nothing can substitute for character, neither reputation nor success. What you are in the dark is who you really are. God sees all and will reward according to his righteous judgment regardless of what others may think.

There are two basic ways of growing in Christlikeness: through your relationship with God in your devotional life of prayer and Scripture, and through the inevitable adversities that will come your way in life.

Many kinds of adversity try the souls of God's shepherds including conflicts in ministry; life crises such as sickness, death, and accidents; financial distress; and undesirable assignments. The question will frequently arise, "Can God be in all these adversities?"

Every Christian leader must learn to see life in terms of the bigger picture, knowing that God in his sovereignty uses many things to develop our character and expand our ministry. "For *we are his workmanship*, created in Christ Jesus for good works, which God prepared beforehand, that we should walk in them" (Ephesians 2:10, emphasis mine). God is the Master Potter and he is shaping us and moulding us to be more Christlike and holy so that we can do the good works which he has planned for us to do.

"And we know that *in all things God works for the good* of those who love him, who have been called according to his purpose" (Romans 8:28, NIV, emphasis mine). This is a tough message to accept, but we believe with unwavering faith in the goodness and faithfulness of God that he sovereignly plans our lives for our good and his glory, including adversities that come our way.

Growing through Others

We are not alone, nor do we grow on our own. We need one another. Seek out a prayer partner, someone to whom you can pour out your heart and unburden your soul. Depending on your location and ministry, this can be a challenge. But you will grow stronger if a prayer partner is in your life.

Seek a mentor, someone whom you admire, and someone from whom you may learn. Observe his or her ministry, visit this person, and discuss your problems and issues with her or him.

It is most helpful if you are accountable to someone whom you can trust and who will counsel you and correct you when needed.

GROWING AS A LEADER IN COMPETENCE

You cannot be a leader with *godly character* alone; you also need *competence*. Half of this book stressed the fundamental need for godly character, but godliness alone does not make a leader. You need competence with skills in order to lead.

According to Robert Clinton (*The Making of a Leader*, p. 201), a biblical leader is "a person [1] with God-given capacity and [2 with] God-given responsibility to influence [3] a specific group of God's people [4] towards [God's] purposes for the group." A Christian leader is *not* a person who simply holds a position called "leader," but someone whom God has *gifted* to be a leader. This gifted person has also been *called* to exercise *influence over a group of people* toward *achieving God's glory and purpose*. In other words, a Christian leader must be *competent* to lead.

Self-Examination

The question is: "As a gifted person called to exercise influence over others, are you growing in competence?" Answers to the following questions will indicate strengths and weaknesses in your leadership skills.

1. *The Gifts Principle:* Am I aware of areas where I am gifted and those areas where I am lacking? Do I recognise those areas where I am lacking in needed gifts for leadership and have humility to accept this limitation?
2. *The Team Principle:* Am I consciously developing a team of workers who can complement each other in fulfilling our dream? Do I seek advice from others? Do I fear their strengths? Do I delegate responsibilities?
3. *The Relational Principle:* Do I have a trusting and cordial relationship with every member of my team? Does everyone feel comfortable in talking with me? Am I seen as a friend? Do I communicate frequently?
4. *The Vision Principle:* Am I future oriented? Do I plan for the future? Am I driven by a God-given vision of future accomplishments?
5. *The Implementation Principle:* Am I able to take a vision and measurable goals and implement them practically? Am I a great dreamer with big ideas but poor at implementation? Can I motivate others to work?

Following are some suggestions to help you grow in leadership competence.

Growing in Competence through Education

Education is no substitute for gifts of leadership. But giftedness without education is a squandering of talents given by God.

Leadership training comes at different levels ranging from one-day seminars to correspondence courses, online courses to residential studies, individual college courses to college degrees.

As a leader, you need appropriate training for the calling God has given you. Formal education, unrelated to your calling, can lead you away from God's will.

Christian leaders can also be over-trained with college and university degrees to the point that they are unable to minister effectively to their people.

Growing in Competence through Experience

Training limited to the classroom will never make a leader. The best form of leadership training is field experience that is built on some kind of formal education. We learn best by doing and we learn from our mistakes.

- *Learn by doing.* Seeking a mentor to coach you in your leadership position is desirable. Even if a full-blown mentoring relationship is not realized, a young leader may visit colleagues to seek advice and gather tips.
- *Learn by applying lessons from school.* If a course on leadership or management was taken in Bible School or College, review the notes frequently. Learn and apply in practice the theory taught in the classroom.
- *Learn from every ministry task.* Learn from every opportunity of service given to you. Test your gifts and potential in those tasks assigned. The more you do, the more your confidence will grow. Be ever faithful. As Christ taught: "Well done, good and faithful servant! You have been faithful with a few things; I will put in charge of many things" (Matthew 25:23, NIV).
- *Learn from negative experiences.* Never assume that you will not make mistakes. When mistakes are made, humility will go a long way in restoring faith. You may forget the notes crammed for a test in school, but you will never forget the lessons learned by the mistakes you make in the field.
- *Learn your spiritual gifts.* Piano lessons cannot teach someone to play the piano if you don't have the musical ability. Neither will a degree in leadership make you a leader if you lack gifts of leadership. Developing God-given gifts is important, but you must first learn what your gifts are.
- *Learn to develop key aspects of leadership skills.* These include people skills in developing relationships, skills in developing a unified team, skills in planning, and skills in implementing the plan.

If you are not good in developing relationships (being people-centred), you cannot become an effective leader. But neither can you be a successful leader without being future-oriented, focusing on goals, and having the ability to implement the goals.

The encouraging truth is this: leadership skills are distributed to most people in varying degrees. You may not be skilled for leading a national team, but you may have skills for a smaller, local team. Let your experience help you develop the skills God has entrusted to you for leadership.

Select Bibliography

Following is a select number of books used in the writing of this volume. The complete bibliography is found in the larger volume, *Learning to Lead.*

Adams, Jay E. *Godliness Through Discipline*. Grand Rapids: Baker Book, 1972.

Adeyemo, Tokunboh. *The Making of a Servant of God*. Nairobi: CLMC, 1993.

Anderson, Leith. *Leadership that Works*. Minneapolis: Bethany House, 1999.

Armerding, Hudson T. *Leadership*. Wheaton: Tyndale House, 1978.

——. *The Heart of Godly Leadership*. Wheaton: Crossway Books, 1992.

Ashford, Ray. *Loving Ourselves*. Philadelphia: Fortress Press, 1977.

Augsburger, David. *The Freedom of Forgiveness*. Chicago: Moody Press, 1970.

Barber, C. *Nehemiah and the Dynamics of Effective Leadership*. Loizeaux, 1987.

Barna, George. *The Power of Vision*. Ventura: Regal Books, 1992.

——, ed. *Leaders on Leadership*. Ventura: Regal Books, 1997.

Boehme, Ron. *Leadership for the 21st Century*. Seattle: Frontline Com., 1989.

Bukusi, Alan. *Thinking Leadership in Africa*. Nairobi, 2004.

Chalke, Steve with Penny Relph. *Managing Your Time*. Kingsway Pub., 1998.

Chima, Alex. "Leadership in the African Church," *AFER*. 26 Dec.: 331–337, 1984.

Clinton, Robert. *The Making of a Leader*. Colorado Springs: NAV Press, 1988.

Cole, Victor. "The Training of Leaders for the Ministry." *African Journal of Evangelical Theology*. No. 2: 33–43, 1991.

Cunneen, Joseph. "Learning from Africa." *Cross Current*. 28 No. 4: p. 385f, 1978.

Eims, LeRoy. *Be a Motivational Leader*. Chariot Victor Publisher, 1996.

——. *Be the Leader You Were Meant to Be*. Wheaton: Victor Books, 1996.

Elliston, Edgar. "Maasai Leadership Development." *Africa Journal of Evangelical Theology*. No. 3: 20–31, 1983.

Engstrom, Ted W. *The Making of a Christian Leader*. Grand Rapids: Zondervan, 1979.

Engstrom, Ted W. and E. Dayton. *The Art of Management for Christian Leaders*. Grand Rapids: Zondervan, 1976.

——. *Managing Your Time*. Grand Rapids: Zondervan, 1977.

Finzel, Hans. *The Top Ten Mistakes Leaders Make*. Wheaton: Victor Books, 1994.

Gangel, Kenneth O. *Competent to Lead*. Chicago: Moody Press, 1974.

——. *Team Leadership in Christian Ministry*. Chicago: Moody Press, 1997.

——. *Doing African Christian Theology*. Nairobi: Evangel.

Gitari, David M. *Responsible Leadership*. Nairobi: Action Publishers, 2005.

Habecker, Eugene B. *The Other Side of Leadership*. Wheaton: Victor Books, 1987.

Harder, Kenneth. "Kenyan Church Leaders." Ph.D. Dissertation, Michigan State University, 1985.

Hocking, David L. *Be a Leader People Follow*. Ventura: Regal Books, 1983.

Janvier, George and Bitrus Thaba. *Understanding Leadership: An African Christian Model*. Jos, Nigeria: published by G. Janvier, 1997.

Kamau, Francis Mugarami. "Toward a Contextualized Leadership Approach for the Pentecostal Church in Kenya." Ph.D. Dissertation, Fuller, 1996.

Kapena, Sumbye. *How to Be a Wise Leader*. Nairobi: Paulines Pub. Africa, 2000.

Kohls, Paul. "A Look at Church Leadership in Africa," *Africa Journal of Evangelical Theology*. No. 2: 107–123, 1998.

Mbogori, Elijah. *Conflict Management*. Nairobi: Evangel, 1999.

Miller, Calvin. *Leadership*. Colorado Springs: NAV Press, 1987.

Mugania, John. "A Study of the African Process of Mediation for Christian Ministry." MA Thesis, Daystar University and Wheaton College, 1994.

Mushanga, Musa. "Church Leadership in a Developing Society." *AFER*. 13 Jan.: 33–40, 1971.

Mutinda, Paul. "Understanding Church Leadership: An Analysis and Assessment of the Africa Inland Church, Kenya." D.Min Dissertation, Biola, 1991.

Mutunga, Stanley. "Contextual Leadership Development for the Church: An Investigation into Rural-Urban Migration to Nairobi." Ph.D. Dissertation, Fuller Theological Seminary, 1993.

Osei-Mensah, Gottfried. *Wanted: Servant Leaders*. African Christian Press, 1990.

Payne, Roland J. "The Influence of the Concept of Traditional African Leadership on Church Leadership." *Africa Theological Journal*. 1: 69–74, 1998.

Richards, Lawrence O. and Clyde Hoeldtke. *A Theology of Church Leadership*. Grand Rapids: Ministry Resources Lib., 1980.

Rush, Myron D. *Management, A Biblical Approach*. Wheaton: Victor Books, 1983.

——. *The New Leader*. Wheaton: Victor Books, 1987.

Spears, Larry ed. *Insights on Leadership*. NY: John Wiley & Sons, 1998.

——. *Servant Leadership: Essays by Robert K. Greenleaf*. NY: Paulist Press, 1998.

Westermann, John. *The Leadership Continuum*. Light House Pub., 1997.

White, John. *Excellence in Leadership*. Downers Grove: InterVarsity Press, 1986.

Wilkes, C. Gene. *Jesus on Leadership*. Wheaton: Tyndale House Pub., 1998.

Wofford, Jerry. *Transforming Christian Leadership*. Grand Rapids: Baker, 1999.

Youssef, Michael. *The Leadership Style of Jesus*. Wheaton: Victor Books, 1986.

Zartman, I. William ed. *Traditional Cures for Modern Conflicts*. London: Lynne Rienner Pub., 2000.

Zokoue, Isaac. "Educating for Servant Leadership in Africa." *Africa Journal of Evangelical Theology*. No. 2: 3–13, 1990.

The Author and His Other Publications

Rev Dr Richard J. Gehman was born in Norristown, Pennsylvania, USA, on December 24, 1935. He earned a Diploma in Theology from Berean Bible School, 1957; a Bachelor of Arts in Anthropology from Wheaton College, 1960; a Master of Arts in New Testament from Wheaton College Graduate School, 1963; a Master of Divinity (MDiv) from Gordon Divinity School, 1963; and a Doctor of Missiology from Fuller Theological Seminary in 1985. He was ordained to the Christian ministry in 1971 by the Bible Fellowship Church.

For 36 years Richard J. Gehman and his wife, Florence (Flo), served in Kenya with the Africa Inland Church (AIC) as missionaries of the Africa Inland Mission (AIM). Throughout those years he became immersed in the rich history of the Africa Inland Church as he engaged in theological education with students, pastors, and teachers throughout the Africa Inland Church in Kenya.

After an initial year of orientation in Kenya, Richard and Florence served at Scott Theological College from 1967 to 1984; and 1994 to 2002. For eight years, 1975–1983, he was principal of the college. He succeeded Dr Mark Shaw as the editor of the *African Journal of Evangelical Theology*, 1995–2002.

He served as assistant pastor of AIC Embakasi, Nairobi, 1985–1987, and as assistant pastor in Maingi, Kijabe, 1987–1994. He launched and coordinated the Theological Advisory Group (TAG), 1985–2002, a research and renewal ministry, and served as the manuscript drafter in the composition of the TAG books.

From the first meeting of the Board of Governors for the Nairobi Evangelical School of Theology, February 1980 until 1994, he served as a member of the NEGST Governing Board. He became the first director of the AIC Training Department, April 1993, and served until December 1994.

In 2002, Richard and Flo retired in the AIM Retirement Center in Florida, USA, where they served in their local church, in their retirement community, and where Richard continued researching and writing. Their son, Nathan, and his wife, Rosanne, have six children and work in the AIM office in Peachtree City, Georgia. Their daughter, Joy, and her husband, Tom, have four children and live in Wheaton, Illinois.

ADDITIONAL BOOKS BY THE AUTHOR

Published by Oasis International Ltd

African Traditional Religion in Biblical Perspective, Revised Edition, 2011.

Learning to Lead: The Making of a Christian Leader in Africa, 2008.

Passing It On: Lessons Learned in Life, 2011 (an autobiography).

From Death to Life: The Birth of the Africa Inland Church, Kenya, 1895–1945.

The Spreading Vineyard: The Growth of the Africa Inland Church, Kenya, from 1945 Onwards (an eBook published in 2017 and available on Amazon.com).

The Spreading Vineyard: The Growth of the Africa Inland Church, Kenya, From 1945 Onwards, 2017 (a shortened version of the eBook), now in print in Kenya.

Overcoming Fear of Death, 2017.

African Christian Theology Revisited, 2018.

Published by Africa Christian Textbooks, Nigeria

African Traditional Religion in the Light of the Bible, 2001.

Published by Evangel Publishing House, Kenya

Doing African Christian Theology: An Evangelical Perspective, 1987

Who Are the Living Dead? A Theology of Death, Life after Death, and the Living Dead, 1999.

Published by Mastoff Press, Morgantown, Pennsylvania, USA

Faith of Our Fathers: From Barbarian to Mennonite and Beyond, 2009.

Published by Scott Christian University, Kenya

(Author served as coordinator and manuscript drafter for the Theological Advisory Group sponsored by Scott Theological College.)

The Roots of Christianity in Africa: Prayer in the History of the Christian Church in Africa (published in English and Kiswahili), 1989.

"Where Two or Three are Gathered . . ." Prayer in the Christian Church in Africa (both a Leader's Guide and a Student Workbook published in four languages), 1989.

"Come, Let Us Bow Down . . ." Worship in the Christian Church in Africa (both a Leader's Guide and a Student Workbook published in English and Kiswahili), 1991.

Worship Guide for Pastors and Elders: How to Improve Worship in the Africa Inland Church (published in English and Kiswahili), 1991.

A Biblical Approach to Marriage and Family in Africa, 1994.

The Holy Spirit and the Church in Africa Today, 2000.

Endnotes

[1] Ted Engstrom, *The Making of a Christian Leader* (Grand Rapids: Zondervan, 1979), 20.

[2] J. Oswald Sanders, *Spiritual Leadership* (Chicago: Moody Press, 1980), 31.

[3] Hans Finzel, *The Top Ten Mistakes Leaders Make* (Wheaton: Victor Books, 1994), 16.

[4] Vance Packard as found in George Barna, *Leaders in Leadership* (Ventura: Regal Books, 1997), 21.

[5] Ewert Cousins, Jean Leclercq, Bernardus Claraevallensis, *Bernard of Clairvaux: Selected Works* (New Jersey: Paulist Press, 1987), 286.

[6] J. Hudson Taylor. *Separation and Service: Or Thoughts on Numbers VI, VII.* (London: Morgan & Scott, n.d.), 47.

[7] 1 Chronicles 29:6-17; Proverbs 3:9f; 10:15; Ecclesiastes 10:19.

[8] Deuteronomy 6:10-12; 8:10-18.

[9] *Ministry of Management* by S. Douglas, B. Cook and H. Hendricks is a helpful book which has been used extensively for this topic of organisation.

34 Characteristics for Godly Leaders

1. Being Attentive to Instruction
2. Practicing Spiritual Disciplines
3. Accepting God's Sovereign Rule
4. Maintaining a Forgiving Spirit
5. Persevering Through Difficulty
6. Choosing Humility Over Pride
7. Showing Humility in Leadership Styles
8. Pracicing Servant Leadership
9. Following the Supreme Model of Humility
10. Developing Godly Self-Esteem
11. Foregoing Jealousy
12. Overcoming Anger
13. Demonstrating Agape Love
14. Following the Supreme Model of Agape Love
15. Practicing Holiness
16. Maintaining Integrity
17. Choosing Purity
18. Displaying Honesty
19. Remaining Pure in Heart
20. Developing the Nature of a *Christian* Leader
21. Adopting the Marks of Effective Leaders
22. Avoiding Mistakes of Christian Leaders
23. Becoming a Change Agent
24. Relying on God While Accepting Responsiblity
25. Refining Management Skills
26. Developing Godly Relationships
27. Becoming a Planner
28. Organising People
29. Shepherding the Flock
30. Developing a Balanced Lifestyle
31. Becoming Self-Disciplined
32. Maintaining Unity
33. Growing in Character
34. Growing in Competence